TO LORD'S WITH A TITLE

The Inside Story of Glamorgan's Championship

HUGH MORRIS
with ANDY SMITH

MAINSTREAM
PUBLISHING

EDINBURGH AND LONDON

To P.L.T. and Melin Dan-Y-Rhiw

First published in 1998 by
MAINSTREAM PUBLISHING COMPANY
(EDINBURGH) LTD
7 Albany Street
Edinburgh EH1 3UG

ISBN 1 84018 072 2

A catalogue record for this book is available from the British Library

Typeset in Bembo
Printed and bound in Great Britain by Butler & Tanner Ltd

Contents

Acknowledgements

We would like to thank Don Shepherd, Dr Andrew Hignell, Mike Carey, Brian Jackson, Fred Raffle and Ivar, Dick Richardson, Matthew Fleming, Paul Johnson, Edgar Jessop, Sally Uphill of the *Western Mail*, Huw John, Huw Evans, Patrick Eagar, Steve Lewis of Sports Bookshop, Cardiff, Dave Luxton of Sportspages, London, Bill Campbell and everyone at Mainstream, players and staff of Glamorgan CCC, and county cricketers past and present, without whom . . .

Foreword

There was never much doubt in the minds of those closely associated with Hugh Morris, the newly appointed Technical Director of the England and Wales Cricket Board, that he would occupy high office within the structure of the game at the conclusion of his very successful career. That the situation materialised so suddenly has surprised many who firmly believe Hugh's batting skills have not diminished one iota, and that further honours for both club and country were not beyond his grasp. Confirmation was at hand at Taunton in September 1997 when his glorious innings of 165 formed the backbone of Glamorgan's victory over Somerset which ensured that the championship would rest in Wales for the third time in the club's history.

It provided a much-needed fillip to Welsh sport; success has, sadly, been lacking in recent years. The nation was proud of the achievement. Furthermore, the approach and attitude to the game met with much approval and very few would deny that the team was the best balanced of them all in the Britannic Assurance County Championship.

I was commentating for BBC Wales when Hugh and Steve James completed the winning run that finally brought the title back. Beside me was Peter Walker, who was with me in the 1969 title-winning team, and we shared the emotion of the moment. In 1969 we came from a long way down the table to win the championship and the pressure was only really on us at the very end. In 1997, the Glamorgan team was right up there from the start and then had the huge pressure of having to win the last games, probably with maximum bonus points, to take the title. But to compare the teams, almost thirty years apart, is an impossible task – cricket has changed so much.

Not every youthful sporting prodigy – and Hugh fitted comfortably into that category – continues to progress to the top of his or her chosen profession. But with determination and honing of technique along the way, the summit was reached with style. Whilst at Blundell's School Hugh broke every run-scoring record. He amassed more than three thousand overall, with a thousand and more in his final season. Immediate reward came with tours to the West Indies and Sri Lanka with England Schools. Glamorgan were already aware that they had a fine talent available, and Hugh's long association with the club began at the age of 15 when he represented the second XI.

The eagerly awaited first-team début came in September 1981 against Leicestershire, when, significantly, Alan Jones – a perfect role model – was playing, though he was then coming towards the end of a great career. Later, as club coach, Alan was able to check on the Morris technique and provide guidance when required. By extraordinary coincidence, Hugh's 52nd and last century for Glamorgan equalled the record established earlier by Alan. Hugh rightly took his place among the great left-handed openers in Glamorgan's history. He is there, alongside his coach and the distinguished Emrys Davies who, for so many years, was the 'rock' of the club's fragile batting line-up on either side of the Second World War. Emrys's career also climaxed with a championship win, with the Wilf Wooller team of 1948.

The coveted county cap was awarded in 1985 for a sterling effort of 1,500 runs during the season and in 1986 Hugh inherited the captaincy at 22 years of age, the youngest captain in the history of Glamorgan CCC. Despite the efforts of talented individuals, the team's performances were disappointing but appeared not to affect Hugh's form immediately. By 1989, however, the burden of the captaincy had taken its toll and resignation followed. Fellow left-hander Alan Butcher took over and, with Hugh, formed one of the club's most successful opening partnerships.

The following year, 1990, was an exceptional one for Hugh. A record 2,276 runs were amassed, including ten centuries – another Glamorgan milestone passed. Reward came with the appointment as captain of England 'A' to Pakistan and Sri Lanka that winter. He was first to 1,000 runs in 1991; England's selectors could no longer delay and three full caps were awarded, two against the West Indies and another against Sri Lanka.

In the opinion of many, including myself, he acquitted himself well, especially in the final Test against the West Indies at the Oval, which England won. Despite the formidable pace attack of Patterson, Walsh, Ambrose and the great Malcolm Marshall, Morris and Gooch shared a century opening partnership as a basis for the team's large first innings total and eventual success. A reasonable performance against Sri Lanka and continued reliability failed to convince the selectors and, alas, there were to be no further caps, much to the dismay of his Welsh supporters.

A more experienced and confident Morris regained the club captaincy in 1993 when Butcher's career was sadly terminated by injury. An exceptionally good Glamorgan team, which included the great Viv Richards, enjoyed a memorable season. Apart from finishing third in the county championship and reaching the semi-finals of the Nat West Trophy, they won the AXA Sunday League Championship by defeating Kent in a head-to-head battle at Canterbury on the final Sunday of the season amid the unrestrained joy of the many thousands of Glamorgan supporters present. They had reason to celebrate: it was the first trophy Glamorgan had won since the championship itself in 1969.

Unfortunately 1994 brought anticlimax as the team plummeted to the foot of the county championship table and improved to only 16th in 1995. Hugh scored more than 1,500 runs before relinquishing the captaincy to Matthew Maynard, who led Glamorgan to a third championship in his second season in charge.

It is an adage, often quoted but true, that the game is far greater than any individual and no one is indispensable, but Hugh's departure after scoring more than 18,000 runs will leave a void in Glamorgan's batting line-up. At the same time, some young batsman will be provided with an opportunity to establish a first-team place for himself which, under normal circumstances, might not have occurred for several years.

Glamorgan have always been one of the most personable teams in the championship, and in recent years this has been due in large part to Hugh's affable approach off the field and sportsmanlike attitude on it. Whenever he had a moment he would join us in the BBC Radio Wales commentary box and the conversation would range from politics to cartoons and back again. After departing the box for the dressing-room, the rest of the day would be punctuated by frequent reappearances from Mr Morris in search of gloves, books, bat or papers that he knew he had left somewhere in the ground at some point.

There is no doubt that Hugh is a worthy choice and is eminently suited to succeed in his new post. On the field he has been a model of technical correctness and his fielding has been high class at all times. A healthy appetite for runs supported by monumental concentration and application has been his trade-mark. Away from the action, his virtues include admirable coaching skills and, importantly in the modern game, an easy and natural ability to communicate both with players and the media, prerequisites of his new post.

The loss will be felt by Glamorgan, but the game as a whole will benefit from his appointment to Lord's.

Hugh Morris has much to offer.

Don Shepherd
Glamorgan, 1997

ONE

1969 and All That

There are some images from childhood that remain indelibly imprinted on the memory. In my mind's eye, I see Don Shepherd bowling the final ball of the 1969 season at Cardiff. I can see it more clearly now than in the grainy television pictures they occasionally show of the event. Occasionally? Towards the end of the 1997 season, when we were neck and neck with Kent going for the title, they were rolled out day after day!

Shep, with the casual stroll that is still a characteristic of his today, went back to his mark. Hands on hips, he adjusted his field with calm authority; there was no doubt who was in charge here. The steady approach, the well-oiled delivery; Brian Brain, the Worcestershire batsman, swung hard, but edged to Bryan Davis. The celebration – Shep, arms aloft, walked slowly across to midwicket and in a very dignified fashion performed gentle-manly 'high fives' with his captain, A.R. Lewis. Glamorgan had won their first championship for 21 years. We kept our long-suffering supporters waiting even longer. It was 28 years before we won another and added a line to the record books.

In 1969 I could recite the names of the Glamorgan first XI in batting order. I frequently did, too, as I walked along St Athan Road on my way to Llanfair County Primary School. A name a step: Jones, Davis, Majid; Lewis, Davis, Walker; Jones, Nash, Cordle; Williams and Shepherd. I can still do it today, but ask me for the 1993 side which won the Sunday League (which I captained) and I am struggling to remember. Did Colin Metson bat ahead of Robert Croft then? Was Matthew Maynard ahead

11

of Viv Richards? I would have to look it up to find out. Yet somewhere, I bet, in about twenty years' time, there will be a chap walking to work, murmuring, 'James, Morris, Dale; Maynard, Cottey, Croft; Shaw, Thomas, Waqar; Watkin and Cosker.'

But let's begin at the beginning, or even before the beginning of the season. All through the winter I had been spending a lot of time coaching schoolchildren in indoor nets all over South Wales from Neath to Newport. It helped me to focus on what I was going to do with my life after my playing days were over.

At 33, after five knee operations, it was definitely time to think of the future. My wife Debbi and our twin girls Bethan and Emily had made a huge difference to me. I love the game and have always enjoyed the camaraderie of county cricket, but it is not, as Sir Richard Hadlee once put it, 'a normal way of life'. I owed my family some semblance of normality at least.

Did I want to stay in the game? Yes. If there was a decent playing contract on offer, I would sign it and continue playing for a couple of years; but if another worthwhile opportunity arose, I would have to consider it. I was really enjoying working with youngsters, so perhaps that was the direction in which I should be heading.

You cannot coach ability, but it was so rewarding to help young players realise their potential. Like the 12-year-old at Cyncoed who thought he was a batsman who could not bowl, but who, after a couple of hours in the nets, was turning leg breaks almost as far as Shane Warne. In Romilly School, Barry, there was an 11-year-old girl with a lovely bowling action. One day, I'm sure, she will surprise a few cynical – male, most probably – opening batsmen.

So, as the new season approached, I had more than a suspicion that after 17 years in first-class cricket, this was going to be one of the last. I was absolutely determined that it would be a memorable year. I kept thinking of those subdued scenes of celebration as Glamorgan won the 1969 title. If we could do it in 1997, we were likely to be far more raucous.

Times were a-changing and not just for me but for Glamorgan too. For 1997, a few familiar faces had gone, including, after 16 years at the club, Steve 'Basil' Barwick. A latter day Shep with his demon off-cutters, seemingly innocuous from the boundary edge, yet Basil reduced some opposition dressing-rooms to dens of fear. Kent always wanted to know if he was in our side – they never fathomed him.

Lancashire were always worried about him too. At Colwyn Bay in 1994, Neil Harvey Fairbrother, one of the best attacking batsman in the country, spent an hour on nought as he found himself trapped at one end, facing Basil. Eventually, he slogged him over mid-off for a single and immediately went LBW to Roland Lefebvre at the other end. Lancashire held a team meeting on the Saturday night to come up with a policy to use against him the next day in the Sunday League. With Lloyd, Watkinson and Wasim in their side as well as Fairbrother, they thought giving him the charge and slogging would be the best option. It worked for the first three overs as Basil went for 29. Off his full eight, he took four for 38.

The next year at Old Trafford, we called Basil in for one of his rare first-class games that summer. I was talking to Harvey, whom I have played with and against since our schooldays, when I noticed that he was transfixed by the sight of the tall, curly-haired figure of Basil climbing out of his car. An hour or so later I was in the nets, facing Basil, when I turned round to see Harvey studying us closely. He was hoping to pick up a few hints from a fellow left-hander of how to cope with Basil and his persistent accuracy. 'It's no use watching me, Harvey,' I shouted, 'I can't hit him off the square either!'

Sure enough, the next day it was: 'Fairbrother, caught Watkin, bowled Barwick, 14'.

Basil was never a great one for training of any sort. A fag and a pint would do nicely for him. He came on our pre-season tour to Zimbabwe in 1993 not having bowled a ball for six months. The nearest he'd got to sport during the winter was a game of darts in his local in Neath. In the nets at Harare he picked up a ball and, with his first three deliveries, knocked back the off stump every time. 'That'll do,' he said. 'That's my pre-season training done with!'

Ottis Gibson, our overseas player from Barbados, had gone

too, and had been replaced by Waqar Younis. I was only acquainted with the great Pakistan quick bowler from a distance of 22 yards – not the ideal position to assess someone's sociability. I did know that he was as fast as any I have faced – pick from Curtly Ambrose, Malcolm Marshall and Allan Donald. It was good to have him on our side.

David Hemp had not enjoyed much of a run in 1996. This was partly my fault, as I had collided with him when fielding at Fenners in the first match of the season. He broke four ribs and punctured a lung, so he played in only five championship games for us and at the end of the season opted to augment the already powerful batting strength at Warwickshire.

We had a new coach, Duncan Fletcher. He captained Zimbabwe in the 1983 World Cup when they won that memorable victory over Australia at Trent Bridge. He became cricket manager of Western Province in South Africa in 1993 and revitalised their side. I did not know him at all. I did not play in the Glamorgan game against South Africa 'A' – managed by Duncan – that season. They beat us by an innings, and maybe that's what impressed the committee. More likely, though, they had studied his record at Western Province where he had been responsible for the development of players like Brian McMillan, Paul Adams, the Kirstens and Craig Matthews. He certainly seemed to have all the right credentials.

Apart from 1993, when we ended up third, Glamorgan had only finished in the top half of the table twice since 1970. It was not an impressive record. In 1996 we had not fulfilled our potential – coming tenth in the championship, knocked out in the first round of the Nat West Trophy and out of the Benson & Hedges Cup at the quarter-final stage. Our season was effectively over halfway through. We scored plenty of runs but we just did not have sufficient back-up strength in the bowling to comple-ment the consistency of Steve Watkin and Robert Croft. Now, with Waqar, who has the best strike-rate of any fast bowler in Test cricket, things were expected to be very different.

Matthew Maynard had taken over the captaincy from me for 1996. He had previously been in charge towards the end of the 1992 season when Alan Butcher was injured. Being captain is a tough job. I had two spells as skipper, from 1986 to 1989 and then from 1993 to 1995. My own personal form suffered on a couple of occasions because of the weight of responsibility and, eventually, at the end of the 1995 season, I decided to concentrate on batting. The press announced this decision as one taken at the end of a season of 'relative failure'. I suppose it was – we were 16th in the championship and had been bottom the year before – but we had also reached two one-day semi-finals in the past three years; prior to that, Glamorgan had only been in two semi-finals in their history. We also won the Sunday League in 1993, but the real problem we needed to address was our failure in the championship. Generally, our cricket did not reflect the strength of our side, especially our batting. Some people in authority at Glamorgan appeared to blame me for the failings. We were trying to re-establish the club after a decade or more of disappointments, yet behind the scenes there were those who did not believe in what we were trying to do and, while not actually deliberately obstructive, did not give the team the wholehearted encouragement we needed.

I thought about moving elsewhere to finish my career, to score a few more thousand runs, maybe on a Test ground, but, in the end, not wanting to uproot the family and still having ambitions to achieve at Glamorgan both for the club and myself, I decided to stay and I've never regretted that decision.

Going into 1997, we had all the right ingredients to achieve success. Perhaps we were still lacking in reserve strength and depth, particularly bowling, but if the 'old sweats' did their job we had a couple of youngsters who could flourish in a winning side. Alun Evans had been given a few opportunities as a batsman in 1996. Now, with the departure of Hemp, he had to put pressure on the batters already established in the side and force his way in. He was the MCC Young Cricketer of the Year in 1995. His coach, Clive Radley, sent him back to Glamorgan from Lord's saying that there was nothing more he could teach him – he now had to glean experience in the first-class game. First, though, he had to get into the side, and ousting one of our top six was not going to be easy. We were all willing to help young players, but we were all professionals.

Dean Cosker was an outstanding prospect. Only 19, a product of Millfield School, he had played for England at Under-15, Under-17 and Under-19 levels. He is a left-arm spinner who has mastered the art of flight, in his bowling at any rate. He was expected to play a major role in tandem with Robert Croft and then on his own in the spin department when Croft went off to the Tests.

Darren Thomas had been labelled 'promising' since he took five Derbyshire wickets in 1992 on his début, but he had never established himself in the first team. During the winter of 1996–97 he was due to develop his game by playing for CBC Old Boys in Pretoria in South Africa, but a last-minute change of mind meant that he spent six months under the guidance of Tom Cartwright back home in Wales. Initially, I was not best pleased because I had arranged Darren's winter abroad with a good friend of mine, the president of the CBC club, Vincent Sinovich. It was to Darren's credit, however, that he worked so hard to change his technique under the guidance of one of the best coaches in the game. Tom spent a lot of time with Darren, improving his run-up and his action while also spelling out to him that to succeed as a professional cricketer he would have to make sacrifices. So out went the burgers and chips and in came pasta and a more determined and professional approach to the game.

Owen Parkin, the right-arm medium pacer, had trouble with injuries, but, fully fit, would be valuable support for Steve Watkin and company. Obviously, Waqar was going to be a huge influence on the young bowlers. He had turned down an apparently larger offer from his previous county, Surrey, to join us, saying that he hoped to emulate Viv Richards who, at Glamorgan, had been such a great inspiration.

One of Duncan Fletcher's first moves was to talk to each member of the playing staff individually to discuss strengths, weaknesses and goals. He asked me at the end of our discussion what I thought he could bring to the club. I said that I felt we had the most talented squad in the 17 seasons I had been associated with the county, and that what we needed most of all was discipline on and off the field and organisation to give us a clear purpose and direction.

Duncan used his business background to set up a management structure within the playing staff. He saw Matthew as the general manager, while Duncan himself was a consultant to him. He asked Matthew to choose three players as senior managers who would act as role models for the team and who would meet regularly to discuss cricketing issues that arose within the club. Tony Cottey, Steve Watkin and I were the three players chosen. It was our job to be the first point of contact for any player who had a problem or wanted to discuss his game or any aspect of the way things were going generally.

Pre-season preparation was also different as, for the first time in a number of years, we did not go abroad for match practice. Previously we had been to the West Indies, Zimbabwe and South Africa. Fortunately, the weather was excellent at home and we had plenty of time outdoors, though we had only two competitive one-day games, against Wales Minor Counties, before the season began for real.

Pre-season training was tough, varied and enjoyable – even including the new 'Phosphate Test' where, basically, you sprint until you are sick! We spent a morning at the University of Wales in Cardiff with gymnastics coach Mitch Fenner to improve flexibility; we had a workshop with a company called Speed, Agility, Quickness which helped us in those departments and we also had several sessions with sports psychologists.

The psychologists dealt with goal-setting, motivation and team work. We were asked what qualities we thought successful teams had. The replies were along the lines of staying injury-free, good fielding, role awareness, pulling together, winning important games, taking responsibility, self-belief and a hundred other things, all of them very worthy, very right and proper. At the end of it all, Duncan simply asked, 'And what about enjoyment?'

Of course he was right and the pre-season we went through was probably the most physically demanding I have ever experienced, but I loved every minute of it.

A lot of emphasis was placed on fitness, but this was achieved through drills with a ball. We were introduced to a number of fielding exercises, designed by Duncan, to improve our fielding under pressure.

The only incident which disturbed us during the pre-season (apart from Robert Croft coming back from Zimbabwe and New Zealand and regaling us *ad nauseam* with tales from the England camp) was when news came through from Pakistan that Waqar had broken down with a stress fracture of the foot on the tour of Sri Lanka and was liable to be out of action for months. A deep and sudden depression descended on the dressing-room. It was broken when Duncan, no doubt sensing the mood, came up with the perfect antidote: 'Sod 'em all,' he said, 'we'll bloody well spin them out!' It lifted the gloom for a while – until we realised that we had only two spinners, one of whom would be required by the England team on a regular basis and the other by England Under-19s. The thought of Cottey and Morris operating in tandem at the Oval in early September was hardly likely to enhance our championship prospects.

When the 1997 edition of *The Cricketers' Who's Who* was published, everyone started talking about the proposal in the book's introduction that the county championship should be revamped into two American Football-style 'conferences' of nine teams each, playing each other once, plus another four counties from the other division. Then the top four from each division would play off in quarter-finals and semi-finals, culminating in a grand, end-of-season finale over five days at Lord's. Lord MacLaurin, the chairman of the England and Wales Cricket Board, who was preparing a blueprint for the future of the game, was told in the press that he ought to pay some attention to the proposal. Just about everybody, it seemed, had an opinion on it. The media asked everyone about it – except me. And I wrote it!

Whenever I had a spare moment I was reading John Arlott's *Gone to the Cricket*, his diary of the 1947 season in England. There is a lovely account of the Glamorgan versus Worcestershire match at Ebbw Vale. Some of the great names of Glamorgan cricket are mentioned, the year before they won their first championship in 1948. Wilf Wooller, of course, as well as Emrys Davies, Arnold Dyson and Allan Watkins. He even names the river correctly – Ebbwfach. I remember one *Test Match Special* commentator in 1993, down to report a Sunday League match, shouting across to Don Shepherd who was working for BBC

Radio Wales from a table by the boundary. 'Shep,' he called, 'what's the name of the river here?'

Shep, with a resigned expression, shouted back, 'Where are you?'

With a nervous fingering of his tie, the man from London replied, obviously puzzled, 'Ebbw Vale.'

Shep paused for a moment before suggesting that if he was in the Thames Valley he would know exactly which river flowed by.

Cricket folk know that 1947 was the vintage year of Compton and Edrich. How poignant that Denis Compton, fifty years on, should die on St George's Day just before the season started.

I like Arlott's opening words to the book: ' "No, he's not at home, he's gone to the cricket," my mother used to say. Now my wife uses the same words.' Just like our house. When I was young, my mother, if she was not actually ferrying me to a game in her MGC, would say something similar to callers; nowadays, Debbi does much the same and also explains to Bethan and Emily who know only three reasons for leaving the house – shopping, holidays and cricket.

I am a man for targets. As the season approached, I was working out exactly what I expected of myself and the team. Overall, for Glamorgan, we had to win the championship and reach a one-day final. Those were my 'outcome' goals. My 'performance' goals to help achieve the outcome were 1,500 runs in the championship, including six centuries. This would take me to fourth in the list of Glamorgan's aggregate run-scorers and would also take me past Alan Jones's record of 52 centuries for the club. I also wanted a hundred against Surrey, which would mean I'd scored a century against every county at first-class level.

I looked briefly at my 1982 *Wisden* for the scorecard of the first game I played in county cricket, against Leicestershire in September 1981. I was 17. I had another year to go at Blundell's School, but there I was on the same page as David Gower and Andy Roberts, so I must have been on the same field. Sure enough – 'caught Gower, bowled Roberts, 16'. With some surprise, I realised that I was the only one of the 22 who played in that match still in county cricket. Checking even further, I found that only a handful of similar vintage were still in the game, and mainly batters too: Athey, Barnett, Gatting, Gooch, Lynch, Moxon and Robinson, with the bowlers represented only by Parsons and Small. A moment earlier I had been a teenager again; now, suddenly, I felt all of 33.

There is no other feeling like the start of a new season: spring scents in the air; the anticipation of playing again; recalling triumphs and achievements; and that curious feeling of 'optimistic trepidation' when scanning a new fixture list. At the top of ours – Warwickshire.

With Allan Donald back, they were a formidable side. In one-day competitions, they knocked us out of the Nat West in 1995 at the semi-final stage and from the Benson & Hedges in the 1996 quarter-final. They always seemed to play well against us and we always underachieved against them.

I spent a lot of time before the Warwickshire game playing mind games, reminding myself of my best innings against them. In 1989 at Swansea I made 108 and at Edgbaston 133. In the opening match of the 1987 season I made 115 and 105 and, even though it was ten years ago, I replayed the innings over and over in my mind, especially the good shots off Donald. Gradually, I built up my confidence for the challenge ahead.

Even so, I distinctly remember the evening before the season started. In the Vale of Glamorgan it was warm and still. The twins were fast asleep in bed. Debbi and I shared a bottle of chilled Chardonnay, but the prospect of facing a fully charged Allan Donald at eleven o'clock the next morning warned against refilling the glass for a third time. I was ready to go 'over the top'.

TWO

Crusted

Glamorgan v Warwickshire
Sophia Gardens, 23–26 April 1997
1996 Britannic Assurance County Championship

		P	W	L	D	Bt	Bo	Pts
1.	LEICESTERSHIRE	17	10	1	6	57	61	296
2.	DERBYSHIRE	17	9	3	5	52	58	269
3.	SURREY	17	8	2	7	49	64	262
4.	KENT	17	9	2	6	47	52	261
5.	ESSEX	17	8	5	4	58	57	255
6.	YORKSHIRE	17	8	5	4	50	58	248
7.	WORCESTERSHIRE	17	6	4	7	45	60	222
8.	WARWICKSHIRE	17	6	4	7	39	55	218
9.	MIDDLESEX	17	7	6	4	30	59	213
10.	GLAMORGAN	17	6	5	6	50	43	207
11.	SOMERSET	17	5	6	6	38	61	197
12.	SUSSEX	17	6	9	2	36	58	196
13.	GLOUCESTERSHIRE	17	5	7	5	23	59	177
14.	HAMPSHIRE	17	3	7	7	41	56	166
15.	LANCASHIRE	17	2	6	9	49	52	160
16.	NORTHAMPTONSHIRE	17	3	8	6	36	57	159
17.	NOTTINGHAMSHIRE	17	1	9	7	42	52	131
18.	DURHAM	17	0	12	5	22	60	97

The Lord's fixture computer could not have given us a tougher
start to the season. The only consolation was that the favourites

for the championship were playing us on our own ground. It would have been a bonus if we could have deployed Waqar against their powerful batting line-up, but he was at home in Pakistan nursing that injured foot. In the dressing-room everyone was trotting out the old adage 'We've got to play them some time'. That was true and, yes, I agreed that they might be more vulnerable at the start of the season rather than later, when they had murdered a couple of the weaker counties and were at the top of the table with a position and reputation to defend. Even so, I would have preferred not to have to meet them first up. After all, we had not even had the benefit of a gentle outing at Fenners or The Parks. No five-hour century against student bowlers under my belt, so no way of knowing whether I was in form or not. As it was, I did feel very fit, as fit as I had been for years. The knees were giving me no trouble, which was very pleasant to report. Even more remarkably, I had trimmed about half a stone off my already sylph-like figure and also sliced a considerable chunk off my two-mile record in training. I could now keep up with Robert Croft in the sprint sessions at least.

When the opposition has a good fast bowler in their ranks, there is always a discernible change in the mood of the dressing-room. In some corners there tends to be a buzz of nervous anticipation. Elsewhere there is silence. Allan Donald (or 'Rocket Man' to his team-mates) was back with Warwickshire after a year off from county cricket. He is more than a good fast bowler – he is an outstanding player. In 1995, on his previous visit to Cardiff for a championship game, we were 86 behind on first innings and thought that we might be able to set them a reasonable target to win the match. Donald came powering in before lunch on the second day and took three wickets for no runs in nine balls. He bowled me with a slower ball that was still quick enough to knock the off stump out of the ground. Steve James and Matthew Maynard were both caught at the wicket in that spell. By the end of the second day, we had been well beaten.

Occasionally, some people wonder if I was mad because I opened the batting against fast bowlers of the capability of Allan Donald. I always felt that it was a great challenge and when I performed well I gained a huge amount of satisfaction that put me on a high and gave me confidence for the next encounter. The other advantage is that being out in the middle, the 'oohs' and 'aahs' of the rest of the team and the comments that issue nervously from them as they watch a ball whistling past a batsman's nose cannot be heard and so cannot upset your concentration. I would much rather be an opener than a number three or four. The players' balcony at Cardiff is a particularly disconcerting place to watch from as, being side on, the bowling looks twice as fast.

Donald was not the only one to worry about in the Warwickshire attack. Gladstone Small has always been a fine bowler, and Tim Munton for some reason has always been underrated.

To be honest, I hated playing against Munton. He was the perfect foil for Donald. After having the ball zipping at you throat-high at one end, some relief was needed at the other. Tim never gave me that luxury. Early in his career he tended to bowl the ball across me and, as long as I knew where my off stump was, I was very comfortable with that. Then he learned how to nip the ball back into me and, using his full height of six foot six, he proved a real handful.

That Wednesday morning I looked out of the dressing-room window and watched the Warwickshire players limbering up out on the field. After a quick head-count I was relieved to see that Tim was not playing. I subsequently learned that he had a long-term back problem. I was disturbed to hear that. I respect him enormously as a bowler and he also happens to be one of the nicest blokes on the circuit.

Tim played an important part in Sri Lanka on the England 'A' tour of 1991–92. Like all of us, he suffered with the humidity, especially in the day-night game against Sri Lanka 'A' at the Khetterama Stadium in Colombo. It was the first-ever match played under lights in Asia and there was a massive crowd there. The air was unbelievably humid – it was a bit like playing in a greenhouse. The coloured kit we had to wear had been manufactured locally, obviously by a company that didn't know what the clothes were intended for, since they all had the texture of heavy woolly jumpers. After six overs of the Sri Lanka innings I was standing at mid-off watching Tim run in to bowl and I could hear the sweat squelching in his boots.

Eventually he walked back to his mark, turned to me and said, 'Hugh, I can see pink elephants!' We hustled him off to the dressing-room for water before he became totally dehydrated. It could never happen at Edgbaston.

Warwickshire won the toss and batted on what appeared to be a good pitch. Cardiff wickets, as a rule, do not seam much but this one did help the bowlers and proved a good toss to lose. In under 40 overs we bowled them out for 151. Sheer delight and amazement at their collapse! Darren Thomas produced an excellent spell. He was so good we did not even think about the absent Waqar. All the hard work during the winter remodelling his action had paid off. The expert tuition of Tom Cartwright had proved invaluable. If Waqar was going to be a long-term absentee, we needed Darren to be quick and more consistent throughout the whole season than he had ever been. To alter a bowler's action radically requires mutual trust from both coach and player. It was highly appropriate that Darren's improvement was first tested against Tom's old county. He played for Warwickshire from 1952 till 1969.

David Hemp's return to Cardiff was unsuccessful. I suppose he was unfortunate to have all the pressure of playing against his former county in his very first game for Warwickshire. Robert Croft came on first change and caught and bowled him with his first ball. Hemp was immediately offered some advice by his former team-mate: 'You should have stayed with us, Hempy, I think your batting's gone off with them!'

David would, I feel, benefit from a more phlegmatic approach to his game. He is intensely ambitious and a perfectionist. This is no bad thing, but instead of wanting to hit every ball he faces with the middle of the bat and being irritated when it sometimes finds the edge, perhaps he should adopt the opening batsman's way of thinking: that when a ball from a quick bowler flies away through the slips for four, the bowler is more likely to be upset than the batsman and maybe the next delivery will be a long half-volley that can be creamed away through the covers for a boundary. I have always thought David had terrific talent and I hoped the brave decision he made to move to Edgbaston would bring him the success he deserves. After all, I felt partly responsible for delaying his progress after the collision at Fenners in 1996.

Robert Croft had returned from the England tour brimming with confidence. He was bowling better than I had ever seen him, at a good pace, accurately and spinning it considerably after employing a change of grip.

Matthew Maynard wanted Adrian Shaw behind the stumps rather than Colin Metson. Runs were required from that position, especially if Waqar was to be available. Matthew regarded Waqar as a bowler who had replaced an all-rounder, Ottis Gibson. It was a decision that the management group supported for cricketing reasons, but the two men 'up top' – Duncan and Matthew – were the ones who came in for most criticism.

Some of Colin's displays behind the sticks had been outstanding in recent years. The gist of the criticism which came from sections of the committee and members was basically that it was callous to discard Metson once we needed a few more runs. They felt that his job was keeping wicket and, while he was still extremely good at it, why drop him?

I am usually nervous before I go in to bat. On the rare occasions when I am not, I do not feel right; I have become so used to that edgy, jittery feeling. Even when I am playing in a friendly or a club game, I feel the same. I have a responsibility to perform and I want to live up to it. I am a creature of habit and superstition. I always change in the same place, put my kit on in the same order and prepare myself mentally in the same way.

Prior to this season, I had opened the innings with Steve James about 150 times, even more often than with my previous partner, Alan Butcher. That was a successful pairing, resulting in over 6,000 runs at an average of nearly 60, with 25 century stands. Although the partnership with Steve was less successful statistically, it was more comfortable personally. It took time to build up the necessary level of understanding but gradually it developed to such an extent that running between the wickets became instinctive. Frequently, we did not have to call for a run, just a look was enough.

Steve is just as superstitious as I am. The routine before we went out to bat did not change in years. I would be outside the dressing-room alone, collecting my thoughts. He would be inside, stretching, loosening up and mentally preparing himself. He always left the dressing-room first to be first onto the field, and on the way he had to thump the ceiling at the top of the stairs, while I had to tap the wall five times with my right glove.

Steve also always took the first ball, but then he was the junior partner! He once said of the routine, 'It's absurd! We know it is. But we know if we change, we'll be out of form forever.'

On the way to the wicket, we just exchanged remarks, muttering, 'Be positive' or 'Good running' and simply 'Good luck' to each other. In between overs the conversation, often the subject of much conjecture from cricket commentators, was rarely more than 'Keep concentrating', 'Don't give it away' and 'Keep going'. Once we were out, it was the mutual consolation society in session. It was either the best ball bowled all day or the worst umpiring decision in the history of the game.

We were allowed such indulgences, according to Steve, because we were the brave souls who went out into the front line of the battle. The ones who had to bat for twenty minutes at the end of the day after an exhausting couple of sessions in the field. Either that, or we are the most expendable members of the side! In recent years, with the advent of four-day cricket, we might have fielded for a day and a half before being asked to bat against a quick bowler who has been sitting in the shade, psyching himself up by doing nothing more strenuous than picking winners from the racing page.

Despite the lack of competitive practice, it was a great start to our season: 190 for the first wicket. Our 14th century opening partnership and our second in succession of 190 or more – we had put on 199 in the last match of the 1996 season at Chelmsford. Everything was in place. We had lost none of the old rapport and, as usual, Steve ran brilliantly between the wickets. When he was out towards the end of the first day, Steve Watkin came in as nightwatchman. Watty's batting is not especially aesthetic – in fact, it was once described as being akin to watching a giraffe at a watering-hole – but the days when we had three genuine number 11s in the side had gone. Steve had worked hard at his batting during the winter against a bowling machine. His new technique enabled him to see off the threat of Allan Donald on the second morning for an hour and a half, a great psychological boost to the rest of the team and especially to me. We added 59, Watty made 18 and I reached a hundred, the fifth time in six seasons I had scored a century in the opening game.

I could not have done it without Watty. Donald's opening spell, seven overs with the wind behind him, was rapid and accurate. I faced only 15 balls, one a yorker from around the wicket that I jabbed down on and only just kept out. Watty was moving into line as Donald, even on such a docile wicket, was whipping them through chest-high. We took only six runs off those seven overs but we did not get out and, importantly, Steve loved every minute of it, though he omitted to tell me that at the time.

Watty is always ready to argue that batting is the easy part of the game. 'Batting is for the glory boys while the bowlers have the toil and sweat of bowling up the hill, into the wind, through the long grass and then the batters drop all the catches.' It is ironic that the only time Steve has been injured in virtually his whole career was whilst batting in the West Indies. He acted as a nightwatchman for England against an Antiguan XI at St John's, scored 45 in three hours but then seized up at the crease. When he hops onto his hobby horse about how easy batting is, I remind him of the strain of batting all that time for a paltry 45.

Adrian Dale played brilliantly, once hitting the left-arm spinner Ashley Giles over the stand and into the River Taff. Warwickshire gave us enough loose deliveries to pull and cut and we put on 242 for the third wicket.

I batted over nine hours and was 233 not out – a career best, better than the 202 not out I had scored in the first champion-ship match of 1996 against Yorkshire. More targets were in my mind – Steve James had made 235 against Notts at Worksop, Matthew Maynard 243 against Hampshire in 1991, the highest score for the club since the war. They were in my sights, while further ahead was the outright club record of 287 not out set back in 1939. Allan Donald had not taken a wicket for about 24 hours but he was back on, bowling as ferociously as ever. He is a great fast bowler not only because of his pace and accuracy, his rhythmic approach and action, but also because he never gives up. I hit him away for four runs and told myself, 'The next one is going to be quick.' And it was.

I saw the length of it and went to duck but it did not bounce as much as I expected. I have been hit before on the helmet by fast bowlers including Ambrose, Walsh and Clarke, but never with such force. It hit me behind my right ear, half on the helmet and half on the bottom of my skull, and rebounded straight back down the pitch to the feet of non-striker Matthew Maynard.

I went down and remember taking my helmet off. It was dented. The side of my face went numb, I had pins and needles around my eyes. My vision became blurred. I tried hard to stay conscious as stumps, fielders' boots, bat and umpires slipped in and out of focus. I went into shock, as though I was frozen stiff. I was carried off and went to Cardiff Royal Infirmary for an X-ray. I was discharged later that evening, but I felt sick and disorientated for days afterwards, even to the extent of recognising Allan the next morning and, when he asked how I was, thinking what a good bloke he is!

A former Glamorgan player phoned up home to ask after me. 'Oh, I think he'll be okay,' said Debbi 'they've X-rayed his skull and found nothing there.'

'What, nothing at all?' he asked.

'No, nothing,' she replied.

By the next morning this news was being passed on around Sophia Gardens with a knowing smile.

I was lucky. It proves that great fast bowlers will always produce the unexpected. Gough and Cork in the past had also pinned me at Cardiff. It is a difficult pitch on which to play fast bowling because it is so hard to judge how high the short ball will actually bounce. If I had not been wearing a helmet I would have been in a terrible mess. The Glamorgan physiotherapist, Dean Conway, thinks that it might have been a life-threatening blow. As it was, I was fit enough to play in the next game, against Essex in the Benson & Hedges Cup at Chelmsford, and score 67.

As a footnote to the incident with Allan Donald, perhaps it might never have happened if Glamorgan's plans ten years earlier had come to fruition. The idea was, at the start of the 1987 season, to play the Indian all-rounder Ravi Shastri on the slow pitches in Wales and elsewhere, and when on the faster tracks bring in an overseas pace bowler. I was in South Africa the winter after my first season as captain and reported back that Donald, then a 20-year-old rookie fast bowler with Orange Free State, was just the man we were looking for. Warwickshire's spies, however, had already noted him and they were in first. We signed Corrie Van Zyl instead. Unfortunately, he suffered with injuries and we never saw the best of him. Warwickshire, meanwhile, have had exceptional value from Donald.

The match itself with Warwickshire petered out to a draw as rain intervened. We had no doubt we would have won comfortably if only we could have retaken the field, but it was not to be.

Warwickshire 1st innings

Moles	c	Shaw	b	Thomas,	9
Khan	c	Shaw	b	Watkin	6
Hemp			c&b	Croft	9
Ostler			c&b	Croft	14
Penney	c	Shaw	b	Thomas	16
Piper	c	James	b	Watkin	1
Smith	c	Shaw	b	Thomas	36
Welch	c	James	b	Thomas	3
Giles	c	Shaw	b	Watkin	29
Donald		not out			20
Small	c	Maynard	b	Butcher	0
Extras					8
Total: all out-39.4 overs					151

Fall: 1-9, 2-19, 3-35, 4-42, 5-43, 6-80, 7-96, 8-97, 9-148

	O	M	R	W
Watkin	11	4	32	3
Thomas	12	1	62	4
Croft	13	2	37	2
Dale	1	0	2	0
Butcher	2.4	0	14	1

Glamorgan 1st innings

James			b	Donald	83
Morris		retired hurt			233
Watkin	c	Small	b	Giles	18
Dale	c	Ostler	b	Giles	106
Maynard		not out			20
Cottey		not out			20
Extras					71
Total: 3wkts dec,154 overs					551

DNB: Butcher, Cosker, Croft, Shaw, Thomas

Fall: 1-190, 2-249, 3-491

	O	M	R	W
Donald	33	12	62	1
Small	22	3	80	0
Welch	33	8	135	1
Giles	38	11	116	1
Smith	26	3	97	0
Hemp	2	0	28	0

Warwickshire 2nd innings

Moles		not out			40
Khan			b	Thomas	0
Welch	c	Dale	b	Croft	35
Donald	c	Shaw	b	Thomas	0
Extras					2
Total: 3 wkts 34.5 overs					77

Fall: 1-6, 2-74, 3-77

	O	M	R	W
Watkin	12	3	15	0
Thomas	12.5	3	31	2
Croft	7	4	10	1
Butcher	3	0	21	0

THREE

Small Beginnings, Help from Heroes

The century against Warwickshire was the 49th I had scored for Glamorgan and the 50th of my first-class career. At the start of the season, I was determined to beat Alan Jones's record of 52 hundreds for the club. I am not one of those players that say records do not matter. I am motivated by records and the breaking of them. To score 53 centuries for Glamorgan would be special because Alan Jones was the player who had made most impression on me when I first went to the club for coaching as a schoolboy in 1978.

While I was growing up I watched Alan batting for Glamorgan in that simple, unhurried, left-handed style of his. Often, I would be watching on a flickering black-and-white TV set as he scored runs at Swansea; his innings being recorded on the quaint, almost triangular scoreboard at St Helen's; the commentary, strictly non-partisan, of course, from the great Wilf Wooller. When I joined the Cardiff club, we would practise on the county ground after the close of play in the championship match. I remember arriving with a bag full of kit and watching almost transfixed as Alan, batting for a draw against Somerset, was holding out against Botham and Garner until he was hit by 'The Big Bird' and had to retire hurt.

On my first visit to the nets with the county side, Tom Cartwright, the cricket manager at the time, told me to go over and watch Alan bat for three-quarters of an hour. Having seen him so often from the boundary, I thought there was little more for me to learn about his style or technique, but I gleaned so much from him in such a short time. Small but important aspects like positioning, balance, attitude to practice and attention to detail spelt out the difference to me between the young hopeful, which I was, and the model professional, which he most certainly was. He was a huge inspiration to me and he has had such a profound influence on Glamorgan cricket, first as a batsman and then as a coach. Since that first time in the nets I have always been able to talk to him, and he has always been approachable and ready to advise.

When I arrived at the crease on my championship début, I scratched out my guard and looked up to check the field. The only member of the opposition in front of me was Andy Roberts – he was 50 yards away at the end of his run. Naïvely, I thought the huge gaps would give me a chance to get off the mark and the four slips, two gullies and cover point were too far away to catch any edge. I do not remember anything about my first ball in first-class cricket – perhaps because I never saw it, but maybe because later Les Taylor hit me on the head with a bouncer. Fortunately, I had taken the precaution of wearing a helmet for the first time – borrowed off Eifion Jones. For ever after, I always wore one. It became as natural for me to put on a helmet and a chest guard to face fast bowling as putting on pads and gloves.

After that first innings, I had a word with Alan Jones in the bar. Truly fast bowling was a new experience for me, so how on earth, I asked him, did anyone get used to it? Alan smiled quietly, put down his pint and said, 'You never do. Whoever says they like playing fast bowling is a bloody liar!' And I think he was right. The batsman who came closest to giving the impression of enjoying batting against fast bowling was, in my opinion, Kevin McKenzie, who opened for Transvaal's 'Mean Machine' in the early 1980s. When the 'rebel' West Indian team went over there, the quicks, Clarke, Alleyne, Croft and Moseley, put a bounty on his wicket. But he played them brilliantly, he was a great hooker. David Steele, the Northamptonshire batsman who played for England in the mid-1970s against the likes of Lillee and Thompson, Roberts, Holding and Daniel, was another who never flinched. He was one of the bravest batsmen I ever saw but probably the most unlikely-looking, with his grey hair and spectacles, more accountant than Test batsman.

Nobody would be surprised if Alan Jones was a bitter man. Throughout the 1960s he was one of the most consistent opening batsmen in the game, yet he never had a chance at Test level. There were other opening batsmen around at the time who were good players, though it is difficult to see why the likes of Brian Bolus, Eric Russell and Roger Prideaux earned caps and not Alan. Alan scored runs against touring sides when they played Glamorgan, including a superb 161 not out off Wes Hall and Charlie Griffith when the West Indies came to Swansea in 1966. *Wisden* describes it as his best innings of the season and, as no one else scored more than 56 in the match, I am sure we can safely assume it was.

Yet, with England looking for an opening batsman having tried and discarded Colin Milburn and Eric Russell, they called up Bob Barber for the Fourth Test at Leeds even though, by that stage in his career, he was only an 'occasional' first-class player. Surely Alan should have played.

A belated opportunity did come in 1970 when England met the Rest of the World in a hastily arranged series that replaced the one planned against South Africa, which had to be called off after anti-apartheid protests. Alan opened at Lord's and scored five and nought, caught behind off Proctor in each innings, and that was it, back to county cricket for ever. So it was important for me to play for England, not just for personal achievement but to prove we do breed opening batsmen in Glamorgan – especially the left-handed variety! In fact, with Emrys Davies going in first for Glamorgan in the days before Alan made his début in 1957, the left-handed tradition lasted for 70 years, almost unbroken.

For Alan, the misery of Lord's 1970 was not complete until a few years later when the International Cricket Conference determined that the matches against the Rest of the World were not 'proper' Test matches. Alan could still point to his England blazer and cap, but apparently they were not earned for an official match. It was John Snow who scoffed, 'Of course they weren't Test matches. With Mike Proctor coming in at number nine, they were like no Test match I had ever played in.'

Alan was captain in 1977 when Glamorgan reached the final of the Gillette Cup at Lord's. My mum and dad had taken my brother Andy, sister Suzanne and me to the quarter-final at Cardiff against Surrey. A great day. Glamorgan beat Edrich, Intikhab, Arnold and Co by four wickets and Alan made a typically gutsy 54.

When Glamorgan won through to the final, I pestered my parents non-stop – we simply had to go to Lord's to see Glamorgan beat Middlesex. It was Glamorgan's year, it was Alan's year. My dad, who played a good class of club cricket with Cowbridge and had trials with the county as a batsman-wicketkeeper, needed little convincing and the five of us, now fully fledged Glamorgan supporters, set off for London.

We had seats in the old Tavern stand and I watched every ball, or tried to. There were some from Wayne Daniel that I could not pick up from the boundary at all and I was amazed that the batsmen could play them so coolly.

It was not the most entertaining day's cricket. Like everyone else from Wales, I cheered loudly when Mike Llewellyn hit that gigantic six off John Emburey onto the roof of the pavilion. Alan Jones only made 18. It turned out not to be Glamorgan's year – a five-wicket win for Middlesex and, to this day, Glamorgan have never been back to Lord's for a one-day final.

I was a sports fanatic in my teenage years. I loved cricket but probably wanted to play top-class rugby even more. I dreamed of playing for Wales at the Arms Park rather than for England at Lord's. My heroes in those days were Barry John, Gareth Edwards and Phil Bennett. Within a year or so, though, I had decided to become a double international – rugby for Wales, cricket for England. Nobody had ever done that, but I was stimulated to play Test cricket when another left-handed hero came to my attention – Clive Lloyd.

I did in fact play first-class rugby as a stand-off when I was at Cardiff Institute (UWIC as it is now) and later for Aberavon. In the 1987 season, I played for Newport United, their second team, but by then the knees were giving me trouble and I sensed that I was likely to be more of a success at cricket than rugby. On a cold, windy and wet day, we played Bath at the Recreation Ground. My knees were hurting badly, I was having a poor game, we were about 60 points to nil down and I thought, 'Why am I doing this?'

Glamorgan were concerned that I would be injured playing rugby (they were not wrong) and that I would miss the start of the cricket season. I knew that if I was absent because of playing rugby, Glamorgan were under no obligation to pay me. A choice had to made and, as I had just been appointed captain of Glamorgan for the first time, I opted for cricket. Alan Jones thought it was a good idea. As he put it, 'There haven't been too many double internationals and the last one was Arthur Milton – that was thirty years ago!'

I had won a Wales student cap at rugby in 1984 playing against the immensely gifted Frenchman Denis Charvet. I was supposed to have partnered Robert Jones at half-back but he, along with Ieuan Evans, was called up to the senior team. Ieuan was at Salford University at the time. Fast, with more hair than nowadays, he also, from memory, was a slightly different shape. He had a reputation for knowing every one of Carmarthen's 81 pubs intimately, but within a year or so he was one of the most dedicated of all Welsh rugby players. Paul Thorburn was the reserve stand-off, kept on the bench by my outstanding form that season. I still wonder how it happened. The training sessions for that student international were held at Pontypridd. With those three around, you can imagine how competitive the sessions were.

So it was cricket for me, with hours spent in the nets under the tutelage of Alan Jones. Alan had continued to play until the 1983 season when he retired having scored over 34,000 runs in 23 consecutive seasons. He was still playing when I scored my first half-century for Glamorgan against Sussex at Sophia Gardens in 1982. A year later, in the same fixture, he scored his 52nd and last century for Glamorgan and together we added 102 for the fourth wicket. At the end of that season I hoped that he would stay in cricket and be around the county and, thank goodness, he did, as a coach and later as the head of development. For so many of us trying to make our way in the game from the second XI in the early 1980s, Alan was a teacher and a guide. The best advice I ever had was from Tom Cartwright that day when he suggested that I watch Alan in the nets at Cardiff for a while. From that moment on, I watched him at every opportunity, listened to him and modelled myself on him. I was a better player as a result.

Eight years after he retired, Alan 'reappeared' in a benefit match for Geoff Holmes on a damp May evening in Dafen. The pitch was a typical club 'sticky' – the sort professionals never see in these times of covered wickets. We failed to make a decent fist of batting in such unfamiliar conditions until Alan came out of the pavilion. He had not played in years but he went out there and showed us all how it was done. Playing every ball off the pitch with the minimum of fuss, forward or mainly back, nudging it around for ones and twos and caning the bad ball. His 50 was made so comfortably it put us all to shame for scratching around for so long for so little.

If Alan was the player I looked up to most of all, Tom Cartwright was the man who shaped my game. Ever since I met Tom when I was a 14-year-old playing for the Wales Schools Under-15s against Ireland at Neath, he has been my mentor. He knows my game inside out and was able to spot in an instant what I was doing right and what I needed to be working on. Things went awry in 1989. I was captain, but I was really struggling for form and in the end felt I owed it to the club and myself to relinquish the captaincy and so be able to concentrate on achieving the standards I knew I was capable of reaching.

I spent that winter working under Tom's guidance and the following season I scored over 2,000 runs, including ten centuries. I think that the winter spent with Tom was a watershed in my career. Prior to the 1990 season, I had averaged about 31 in first-class cricket. Subsequently my average has been around 50.

1981–97	18,520 runs at 41.06	
1981–89	6,336 runs at 31.21	
1990–97	12,184 runs at 49.13	

I doubt if I could have made it in county cricket without the grounding I enjoyed at Blundell's. When I first went there, I was homesick and wanted to leave during virtually every moment of the first two terms. I found it hard being two and half hours away from home in Cardiff, and making a new life without my family and friends around me was very difficult. My parents and I talked it through and it was suggested that I stick it out for the first year but if I still felt the same then they would agree to me leaving. My grandfather had been at Blundell's, so it was disappointing all round that I was not enjoying being there, until the summer!

I arrived at Blundell's as a rugby player who could play cricket. Playing every afternoon at the school, on good tracks, was a delight. Sport changed everything for me and though I did not score many runs in my early school matches at least I had a focus for my attentions. From then on, I was very happy there and when my younger brother Andrew came to the school, he had no problems settling down. Even so, I would not send my children away to school if there was the alternative of a good school in our neighbourhood.

In my second year, playing for the junior colts XI, cricket assumed greater importance than rugby. It was probably due to the influence of the Master-in-Charge, Chris Reichwald. He encouraged me to keep wicket and so, at the age of 14, play for the first XI as stumper, batting at seven. In the firsts, we were coached by Terry Barwell, the former Somerset player, born in South Africa, who had just finished playing Minor County cricket for Wiltshire. He stressed the importance of fielding and, having given up the gloves, made me into a decent cover fieldsman. I began to score 50s, then the first century – 127 not out at Sherborne in 1979. Cricket was definitely for me.

For my last two years at Blundell's, David Fursdon was in charge. He had won cricket blues at Oxford University and played for Devon in the Minor Counties. For those two years we were unbeaten. I was captain and relishing our games against the likes of Uppingham with James Whitaker and Jonathan Agnew, who thought they could play a bit.

In 1982, having made my first-class début the previous season, I made over a thousand runs in schools cricket, was captain of

England Schoolboys and played for Young England against Young West Indies alongside David Capel and Jack Russell and against Phil Simmons, Roger Harper and Courtney Walsh. The following summer I was captain of Young England against Australia. Then the likes of John Morris, Paul Johnson, Neil Fairbrother and Steve Rhodes were up against Craig McDermott, Tony Dodemaide and Ian Healy, playing solely as a batsman. It is good to realise that so many friendships forged in those days have stood the test of time, competition and a little good-natured sledging!

HUGH MORRIS AT BLUNDELL'S SCHOOL 1978-82

	M	No	Runs	HS	Avge
1982	15	7	1032	129*	129.00
1981	13	8	923	154*	184.60
1980	13	3	467	81*	46.70
1979	11	4	628	127*	89.71
1978	10	1	319	71	35.44

Of course, I might have made a first-class cricketer without Blundell's, but perhaps not one of such longevity. It did, in the end, make me a stronger, more independent character. At the end of the season I looked up from the middle to the balcony on the pavilion at Taunton. There, alongside my parents, sat Ted Crowe, the godfather of sport at Blundell's who did so much for me during my time there. He was a pretty good Maths teacher too.

Sadly, Ernie Steele, who was a big supporter of mine, died at the start of the season. At school, he had umpired all the matches in which I played. A Yorkshireman, he was the professional at Blundell's and did so much to iron out my technique and prepare me for being a first-class cricketer.

GLAMORGAN IN THE 1997 BENSON & HEDGES CUP

28.4.97 Lost to Essex at Chelmsford by five wickets
     Glamorgan 210 (49.3 overs) Morris 67
     Essex 211 for five (43.1 overs) Irani 82*

30.4.97 Lost to Somerset at Taunton by 141 runs
     Somerset 258 for nine (50 overs) Lathwell 77, Harden 68
     Glamorgan 117 (30.4 overs)

2.5.97 Beat Middlesex at Cardiff by seven runs
     Glamorgan 252 for 7 (50 overs) Morris 76, Dale 100
     Middlesex 245 (49.2 overs) Kallis 72

5.5.97 Beat Ireland at Cardiff by six wickets
     Ireland 202 for nine (50 overs) Cronje 85
     Glamorgan 203 for four (30.3 overs) Maynard 50

It was far from being an impressive B&H campaign with only the win over Middlesex to give us much encouragement. Middlesex became the possessors of an unwanted record as the first county side to be beaten in three capital cities in a week. Earlier they had lost to Essex at Lord's and then, remarkably, gone down to a Hansie Cronje-inspired Ireland in Dublin, before coming to Cardiff.

FOUR

With a Daff on the Chest

Yorkshire v Glamorgan
Headingley, 7–10 May 1997
Britannic Assurance County Championship

		P	Pts
1.	GLAMORGAN	1	11
2.	SUSSEX	1	11
3.	SOMERSET	1	10
4.	LEICESTERSHIRE	1	10
5.	KENT	1	9
6.	LANCASHIRE	1	9
7.	NORTHAMPTONSHIRE	1	9
8.	WORCESTERSHIRE	1	8
9.	GLOUCESTERSHIRE	1	8
10.	ESSEX	1	8
11.	DERBYSHIRE	1	8
12.	DURHAM	1	8
13.	SURREY	1	7
14.	NOTTINGHAMSHIRE	1	5
15.	HAMPSHIRE	1	4
16.	WARWICKSHIRE	1	3
17.	MIDDLESEX	0	0
18.	YORKSHIRE	0	0

Waqar's injury cleared up quicker than even we had dared hope
and he made his Glamorgan début in the Benson & Hedges

Cup. He was welcomed to Wales by all our supporters, desperate for success since Viv Richards left the club. He was with us for the first away match in the championship, at Headingley against Yorkshire in mid-May. Away trips – after 16 seasons of them – tend to be routine. I was rooming again with Steve Watkin. We must be the most boring pair of county cricketers ever when we are away from home. A meal before eight o'clock in the evening or Watty fails to function. It probably has something to do with his blood-sugar levels and bowling about 800 overs a season. A couple of beers follow and then we are transfixed in front of the television in the hotel room – especially if *The X-files* are on. Room-mates are supposed to be compatible, but Watty's insistence on keeping the window open, even on freezing cold Yorkshire nights, does not always meet with my approval.

Glamorgan's record at Headingley was atrocious. It was the only county headquarters where we had never won. Superstition had no place in the new Glamorgan under Duncan Fletcher, though. This, he told us, would be our chance to make history.

Headingley used to be uneven when I started playing. More recently it had flattened out. In 1987 we played Yorkshire at Headingley in the Nat West second round and the game was all over by three o'clock. The pitch produced movement in all directions. We were bowled out for 83 in about two hours by Arnie Sidebottom and Paul Jarvis. Arnie took five for eight in his first seven overs. I batted right through for 16 not out. I have no idea how I managed to survive and everybody else got out. The only reason we topped 80 was because Greg Thomas played with outrageous abandon and hit 33 off 26 balls. As for my innings, *Wisden* described it as 'perhaps the most memorable 16 runs – with as many bruises – of its kind by a Glamorgan player'.

After reading that, Andrew Hignell, Glamorgan's statistician, pointed out that in Glamorgan's early days one T.R. Morgan was particularly adept at carrying his bat. In the 1922 and 1923 seasons he managed to do it four times, including against Yorkshire in 1922 at the Arms Park. It required bribery of a few pints to keep Andrew quiet about Mr Morgan's feats of survival – necessary because Morgan's nickname was 'Tubby' and I was not at all interested in acquiring that particular tag.

The pitch prepared for the championship game had pace and bounce and Darren Gough opened up with a really hostile spell that suggested he was back to his best. The yorker was working again and he troubled Steve and me a couple of times. We put on 86 for the first wicket before I was caught at the wicket off Chris Silverwood. Silverwood had been on the England tour during the winter and played in a Test against Zimbabwe at Bulawayo. He took three for 80 against us but seemed to lack rhythm and tire quickly – though not having played against him before, maybe that was a judgement based on his apparently languid approach.

He is one for the future, provided that he learns from those around him. Not all the advice he will receive during his career will be beneficial. One reporter who covered his first-class début for Yorkshire against Hampshire at Southampton in 1993 suggested that he would generate more pace by extending his run-up. As it was already about 30 yards, Steve Oldham, Yorkshire's then director of cricket, told him to ignore such advice and concentrate on making each stride of the approach count.

Gough's enthusiasm and self-belief could easily rub off on Silverwood and be of benefit. He could also learn from watching the likes of Steve Watkin, whose week-in, week-out professional approach means that he bowls accurately and meanly. Over the past five seasons Watty, in 80 championship matches, has taken over 300 wickets (more than anybody else) at an average of 25.70 (lower than anyone else). Exemplary.

I was pleased with my form in making 55. There were no complications from the Donald incident. Steve James's first hundred of the season was a fine innings, though the way we collapsed from 225 for one to 336 all out was disconcerting. The middle order blamed a lack of match practice and good bowling by Darren Gough.

Gough did bowl well. Four for two in ten balls at one stage. The middle order had not seen much action because the top three had hogged the crease so much. With 142 overs lost on the first two days due to rain, so much of the atmosphere of the match was ruined. It is always difficult to raise the tempo of the game when it is continually disrupted.

Another part of the routine of away trips was the team meal.

Usually, on a Friday night, the team would meet for an established ritual – the awarding of the 'Dick of the Week' shirt and hat. The very embarrassed recipient at Headingley was H. Morris for arriving at the ground with the keys to Gary Butcher's car in his pocket. As his car was in Cardiff, Gary had to make hurried alternative arrangements to travel to Leeds.

Yorkshire's new overseas signing, Darren Lehmann, made his championship début against us and hit a quick 54 off 64 balls, looking the part completely. Twelve fours in his brief stay at the wicket; but he looked certain to provide some rich entertainment for the Yorkshire members during the summer. I had played against him before, in Australia in 1990, when I was called in as 'reinforcement' for the England team after Graham Gooch had gone to hospital with an infected hand. I played against Sir Donald Bradman's Invitation XI at the Bowral Oval. I first noticed the young Lehmann in the field – he ran me out from deep square leg for 50. When he came in, Lehmann, aged only 20 then, showed no sign of being overawed – far from it, as he smashed the England attack of Malcolm, Bicknell and Lewis for 112 not out off 166 balls. With Michael Bevan he added 120 in little over an hour. It was a remarkable display of hitting in front of an excited, sell-out crowd, that confirmed he was likely to be around top-class cricket for a while. It nearly ended prematurely for him, though. Two months after the game at Bowral, he was batting in the nets against a club fast bowler when he pulled a short ball into his face. He was rushed to hospital with a broken cheekbone, and it was feared that his left eye might be permanently damaged. An operation proved to be a success, and in fact, a month later, he was playing in the Sheffield Shield final for Victoria. It seems strange that at the start of his career he was dismissed as having 'occasionally questionable application'.

Lehmann definitely won the battle of the overseas pros when he played against us – Waqar took only one wicket in the Yorkshire innings. It was a glorious sight, though: Waqar running in down the hill at Headingley with the daffodil on his chest. We all felt exhilarated by his appearance and his determination, even though things did not go right for him at the start, especially when I dropped Gavin Hamilton at slip when he was yet to get off the mark. The catch came to me much lower than I expected off a bowler of Waqar's pace. I was just totally unused to Waqar's skidding delivery. I made a mental note to stay down a little longer and also took heart that if I was disconcerted by Waqar in the field, what must it be like for batsmen?

In the second innings I was out, bowled by Michael Vaughan for 96. I was annoyed on two counts – being dismissed four short of my fiftieth first-class century for Glamorgan and by the fact that I regard Vaughan as an 'occasional' off-spinner, so it was extremely disappointing to lose my wicket to him. I learned subsequently that Eddie Hemmings, who is an authority on off-spinners, regards Vaughan as the player with most potential in that department around the counties. He took only 16 first-class wickets in 1996, so they obviously are not in complete agreement with Eddie about his bowling at Yorkshire.

Rain had the final say. We left Yorkshire 303 to win but they did not even start. This was definitely not the result we wanted after the draw we had had to settle for against Warwickshire. In both games we played well enough to suggest that our first championship win would not be far away. The real bonus was a fully fit Waqar making his first-class début for us. Even though the pundits wrote us off at the start of the season as 'outsiders' for the title and rated us only 'possibles' for a one-day competition, we were confident that something would come our way in 1997 and thought that we were likely to be seen at our best in the four-day game.

I picked up a copy of the *Yorkshire Yearbook* at Headingley, a classic of its type, especially for the statistically minded. It is not the usual softback annual that most counties produce, but a pocket-sized hardback with the feel of a prayerbook – highly appropriate considering cricket is a religion in Yorkshire. One line from William Kerr caught my eye, describing an off drive from George Hirst as being 'mellow as brown ale'. By contrast my drives through the offside are usually described as 'clubbed'. I enjoy playing against Yorkshire; I like the way they play the game and I usually score runs against them, which helps. I made my first championship hundred against Yorkshire at Cardiff in 1984, batting for a long time with Rodney Ontong and even facing a few deliveries from Geoffrey Boycott. My mum's mother – 'Nan'

– was sitting in front of the pavilion and at the end of the innings when she congratulated me, Geoffrey came over, said, 'Well done, lad,' and shook hands with Nan, but not with me!

Geoffrey scored an unbeaten century when Yorkshire batted again, but should have been out and become my second first-class wicket – but John Steele at slip dropped the catch.

There has always been an affiliation between Glamorgan and Yorkshire, fostered in recent years by Geoff Lister, an exiled 'Yorkie' who moved to Bridgend for business reasons. A cricket-lover, he is one of our staunchest supporters but also retains his Yorkshire connections. He is now fully integrated into Wales and regards England as merely a stretch of land that separates Wales and Yorkshire.

It is quite a considerable stretch of land between the two as we well know from driving back down the M1 from Leeds *en route* to Cardiff. We heard on the radio that Gloucestershire had become the first county to pull off a win in the county championship, by beating Hampshire at Bristol by six wickets. Syd Lawrence was back in the team after nearly six years away following that horrific knee injury he suffered in New Zealand. Mike Smith, Gloucestershire's left-arm medium-pacer took ten wickets in the match. Watty raised his eyebrows when he heard that; he had not taken ten wickets in a match for two years. He knew he was due.

Glamorgan 1st innings

James		run out			109
Morris	c	Blakey	b	Silverwood	55
Dale	c	Blakey	b	Gough	44
Maynard	c	Byas	b	Silverwood	3
Cottey	c	Blakey	b	Gough	4
Croft	st	Blakey	b	Stemp	57
Butcher			lbw	Gough	0
Shaw			lbw	Gough	0
Thomas	c	Lehmann	b	Gough	2
Waqar			lbw	Silverwood	12
Watkin		not out			18
Extras					32
Total: all out 102.4 overs					336

Fall: 1-86, 2-225, 3-230, 4-237, 5-250, 6-250, 7-250, 8-252, 9-285

	O	M	R	W
Gough	23	9	56	5
Silverwood	23	3	80	3
Hamilton	21	6	63	0
White	13	0	62	0
Stemp	16.4	2	44	1
Vaughan	4	2	6	0
McGrath	2	0	9	0

Yorkshire 1st innings

McGrath	c	Shaw	b	Waqar	14
Vaughan	c	Shaw	b	Croft	25
Byas			lbw	Watkin	8
Lehmann			b	Butcher	54
Parker	c	James	b	Butcher	9
White			lbw	Thomas	25
Blakey	c	Maynard	b	Croft	6
Gough	c	Waqar	b	Croft	28
Hamilton	st	Shaw	b	Croft	11
Silverwood		not out			11
Stemp		not out			1
Extras					8
Total: 9 wkts dec 54.2 overs					200

Fall: 1-14, 2-33, 3-93, 4-112, 5-113, 6-130, 7-172, 8-184, 9-192

	O	M	R	W
Waqar	12	1	42	1
Watkin	12	4	34	1
Thomas	5	0	32	1
Dale	4	0	21	0
Croft	16.2	3	58	4
Butcher	5	1	11	2

Glamorgan 2nd innings

James		b	Stemp	52
Morris		b	Vaughan	96
Dale	not out			10
Maynard	not out			0
Extras				8
Total: 2 wkts dec 40 overs				166

Fall: 1-110, 2-166

	O	M	R	W
Gough	6	0	33	0
Stemp	16	5	35	1
Vaughan	10	1	50	1
Silverwood	5	0	27	0
Hamilton	3	0	17	0

FIVE

Another Canterbury Tale

Kent v Glamorgan
St Lawrence Ground, 14–17 May 1997
Britannic Assurance County Championship

		P	Pts
1.	GLOUCESTERSHIRE	2	32
2.	GLAMORGAN	2	21
3.	SOMERSET	2	19
4.	DURHAM	2	18
5.	WORCESTERSHIRE	2	17
6.	LEICESTERSHIRE	2	17
7.	NORTHAMPTONSHIRE	2	16
8.	SUSSEX	2	16
9.	DERBYSHIRE	2	15
10.	SURREY	2	13
11.	NOTTINGHAMSHIRE	2	12
12.	MIDDLESEX	1	11
13.	HAMPSHIRE	2	10
14.	LANCASHIRE	1	9
15.	KENT	1	9
16.	YORKSHIRE	1	8
17.	ESSEX	1	8
18.	WARWICKSHIRE	1	3

The first month of the season was a demanding schedule of one-night stop-overs for Benson & Hedges matches punctuated with longer stays away for four-day games. The family are used to me dashing out of the house at the last minute to set off to some far-flung county ground only to reappear a quarter of an hour later having reached the motorway and remembered that all my socks were still in the drier.

Two of our longest journeys for championship games were in May – Headingley and then Canterbury, which I reckoned would make Colwyn Bay in August the next longest trip of the season and that would be for a home match!

There are some county grounds that I wouldn't miss if I never play on them again. Canterbury is not one of them. Would I miss the lime tree inside the boundary? I spent a few hours at Canterbury missing it – I never hit it once when I was batting and didn't even see it hit. I would not miss the near incomprehensible scoreboard above the Les Ames Stand. I played one of my best innings on the ground in the Benson & Hedges Cup in 1996 when we had to score quickly and win to qualify for a home tie in the quarter-finals. I hit a hundred off 68 balls and with Steve James put on 181 in 25 overs for the first wicket. I missed the first ball bowled to me by Julian Thompson but, apart from that, virtually everything else flew off the middle of the bat and how rarely that happens. It was a magnificent feeling; as if I were invincible. Everything I attempted came off and we won with time to spare, but I could never work out how many we needed or how many overs were left, so I just carried on hitting.

Canterbury also brings back memories of the win that brought us the 1993 Sunday League title: Viv's last stand, hymns and arias in the Bat and Ball and walking into the dressing-room that morning to see Don Shepherd looking out over the ground. Most of our players were practising on the outfield, and the spectators were pouring in. I was unbelievably nervous. 'Morning, Shep,' I called. He turned round very slowly and, with a grim look, said, 'Canterbury. We never win here.'

Prior to the 1993 season we had finished in the top ten of the Sunday League only three times and never higher than fifth. To win the trophy having won 13 of 17 matches that season demonstrated how much of an improvement we had made, thanks in part to the great contribution from Viv Richards. He wanted to retire from county cricket with a title, and how I know that feeling. We were in the running for the championship itself until Middlesex pulled away from us decisively in August. After losing in the semi-finals of the Nat West at Hove, the Sunday League it had to be. At the start of the season, it was Viv doing it for us, the catalyst of the team, the one we all looked to for approval, for inspiration, for guidance, the one we all wanted to bat with. By the end of the season, we were all pulling for Viv to bow out with another title.

I was batting when Viv came out of the pavilion after a moment's dramatic pause, like a big star deliberately delaying his entrance to create maximum effect. It worked. The crowd rose as one and roared him all the way to the wicket. I was sweating hard and concerned that at 98 for 3 needing 201, the game was going Kent's way. Yet as he strode out to the crease looking utterly imperial, the hairs on the back of my neck stood up. I knew that I would never experience another moment like it. It all affected Viv too. He was on 14 when he swung at a quick bouncer from Duncan Spencer and skied it straight up in the air. I was aghast, and even more so when, in the midst of total chaos, Viv walked down the wicket, thumped me in the chest and said, 'No worries, captain. We're gonna win!' Spencer had overstepped and it had been called no ball.

When we had pulled it off, the dressing-room was a sea of excited faces, a wall of noise. Viv burst through the door screaming with delight, laughing in that high-pitched cackle of his. 'Captain, captain,' he shouted as he grabbed hold of me, 'you will never know how much this one means to me.' In the middle of all that excitement and relief it was the one remark that struck a chord. It was amazing that after having achieved so much in his career, Viv wanted a domestic title so much.

The overseas pros who had played for us since Viv retired had struggled for fitness and form. Ottis Gibson was particularly unfortunate in his short time with us to be hampered by injury and then interrupted by a West Indies tour. The club decided to go for a big-name signing once more in the mould of IVA and plumped for Waqar.

Kent at Canterbury was expected to be a real test of our championship credentials. They have, for as long as I can remember, always been a formidable side, especially in one-day cricket, where they excel, but have not picked up the trophies they deserve. They were possible contenders for the county championship, provided that their battery of quick bowlers remained fit. Headley, McCague, Igglesden, Thompson, and with Fleming usually around too, add up to a series of problems for any batting line-up. On the opening day at the St Lawrence ground on this occasion, Martin McCague ripped through our top order and we were 108 for six before Croft, Waqar, Thomas and Watkin clattered the ball to all parts to give themselves something to bowl at. McCague bowled well on a pitch that provided pace and movement, taking six wickets. After claiming that they never had the chance to bat in anger, the middle order could not complain at not having the opportunity now. In two successive championship matches we had fallen short of our target in first innings. That evening in the Bat and Ball across the road from the main gate of the ground, Waqar was asked by Edward Bevan, the BBC Wales reporter: 'If you can bat like that, you should be further up the order for Pakistan, shouldn't you?'

Waqar grinned broadly (he had made a hard-hit 47). 'Wasim would never agree to that,' he said. 'He thinks he's the only all-rounder for Pakistan!'

At the start of the second day it was Robert Croft who swung the game our way. Matthew had only brought him on to bowl to allow Waqar and Watkin to change ends. Alan Wells was beaten in the flight and LBW, so Croft stayed on and bamboozled another four Kent batsmen. He was in superb form, looking as though he was capable of taking a wicket with every ball. He had excellent control of flight and length, turned it, made it bounce. The tour with England had given him an enormous confidence boost. He went a very good bowler and came back a top-class international.

'Jazzer' Fleming will testify to the amount of zip that Croft produced. In the second innings, the ball was through him and had knocked out his off stump before he was half-way through his stroke. It was not the happiest of innings by Fleming.

Playing forward defensively earlier, he had split his trousers, prompting continual ribald remarks from Steve James at short leg who had an unrestricted view of the honourable gentleman's backside.

Croft's immaculate display encouraged Dean Cosker in the second innings. He removed four of Kent's top six including a beautiful spell at Wells who was threatening to take the game away from us. The evening before, we had a team discussion to outline plans to win the game. Thinking back to 1993 and the Nat West semi-final at Hove, we knew how dangerous Wells could be. Overnight he was 84 not out and Kent, needing 319 to win were about halfway there at 156 for three. If Wells stayed till lunch, Kent would be well placed. Duncan Fletcher had been watching Wells closely and he suggested using Cosker, bowling over the wicket, close to the stumps and aiming into the rough just outside Wells's leg stump, would be the best ploy. Cosker's fourth ball of the day was pitched perfectly; nipping low across pad and bat, it nicked the outside edge and Tony Cottey pouched the catch at slip.

Meanwhile, Waqar was beginning to bowl with pace and rhythm and Dean Headley was a victim of the deadly in-swinging yorker. With Waqar around, we always felt capable of taking three or four wickets cheaply and they were well short at the finish. It proved to be one of the most important wins of the season, since Kent, with their new overseas signing Paul Strang, who took five wickets in the match, and under new coach John Wright, looked likely to be among the top three candidates by the end of the season.

Up until 1993, I had rarely been on the winning side against Kent in any competition. Since the famous Sunday League win, we had an outstanding record against them.

I played little part in the match. I made 18 in the first innings and then, after twisting my ankle playing football on the outfield at close of play, I could not field and batted at six in our second innings. I could not remember batting so far down the order for Glamorgan since the first couple of seasons of my career. I was about to suggest that my presence at number six on a regular basis might help stiffen the middle order. Fortunately,

I kept such tongue-in-cheek remarks to myself. I would have really suffered the whiplash of Adrian Shaw's wit. He had opened with Steve James in my place and they had put on a hundred!

Being off the field for such a long time at Canterbury enabled me to renew my acquaintance with one of my favourite ladies on the county circuit, June Waldron, who has been working in the dining-room at the St Lawrence ground for over ten years now. She is so popular with all the players, home and opposition alike. She always asks after the family and serves up the most delicious banana cake for tea. Extra helpings on the days when I could not field! I must admit, I do have a reputation as a bit of a trencher-man, not quite in the Mike Gatting class but not far off. Gatt, incidentally, is another fan of June's even though she once put the then Middlesex captain out of action when she accidentally tripped and spilt scalding hot tea all over him. Gatt made no fuss at all, probably realising that if he did, one of his favourite tables on the circuit would not be the same again. When he came back from hospital he gave her a big kiss to show there were no hard feelings.

It is people like June who give the county game the pleasant atmosphere it invariably has. There is more to county cricket than just the players.

Glamorgan 1st innings

James			b	McCague	46
Morris			b	McCague	18
Dale	c	Strang	b	McCague	0
Maynard			lbw	Headley	12
Cottey	c	Marsh	b	McCague	17
Croft	c	Fleming	b	Ealham	39
Shaw			lbw	Strang	0
Waqar	c	Marsh	b	McCague	47
Thomas	c	Marsh	b	Headley	46
Watkin	c	Strang	b	McCague	39
Cosker		not out			0
Extras					15
Total: all out 84.4 overs					279

Fall: 1-37, 2-37, 3-71, 4-88, 5-105, 6-108, 7-171, 8-191, 9-249

	O	M	R	W
McCague	20.4	5	75	6
Headley	25	7	74	2
Ealham	15	5	64	1
Strang	21	6	51	1
Fleming	3	0	10	0

Kent 1st innings

Fulton	c	Thomas	b	Waqar	19
Walker	c	Croft	b	Watkin	9
Wells			lbw	Croft	31
Cowdrey	c	Maynard	b	Croft	36
Llong			lbw	Croft	4
Ealham	c	Cosker	b	Thomas	15
Fleming			c&b	Croft	1
Strang	c	Cosker	b	Thomas	1
Marsh			lbw	Thomas	7
McCague	c	Thomas	b	Croft	12
Headley		not out			4
Extras					15

Total: all out 53.4 overs 154

Fall: 1-20, 2-33, 3-68, 4-78, 5-111, 6-113, 7-126, 8-135, 9-144

	O	M	R	W
Waqar	10	3	49	1
Watkin	14	5	46	1
Thomas	11	4	13	3
Croft	18.4	5	33	5

Glamorgan 2nd innings

James			b	Fleming	54
Shaw			b	McCague	30
Dale			lbw	Strang	6
Maynard	c	Marsh	b	Strang	5
Cottey			lbw	Strang	0
Morris	c	McCague	b	Fleming	25
Croft	c	Walker	b	Fleming	29
Waqar			lbw	Fleming	10
Thomas		run out			8
Watkin	c	Marsh	b	Strang	0
Cosker		not out			5
Extras					21

Total: all out 61.5 overs 193

Fall: 1-100, 2-109, 3-109, 4-109, 5-114, 6-161, 7-176, 8-181, 9-186

	O	M	R	W
McCague	12	2	54	1
Headley	7	1	31	0
Ealham	5	3	12	0
Strang	23.5	5	59	4
Fleming	14	4	28	4

Kent 2nd innings

Fulton			b	Waqar	6
Walker			b	Cosker	35
Wells	c	Cottey	b	Cosker	85
Cowdrey	c	Cottey	b	Cosker	29
Marsh	c	Shaw	b	Croft	15
Llong			b	Cosker	15
Ealham		not out			20
Fleming			b	Croft	14
Strang	c	Watkin	b	Croft	3
McCague	c	Cottey	b	Waqar	4
Headley			lbw	Waqar	2
Extras					3

Total: all out 73 overs   231

Fall: 1-8, 2-90, 3-154, 4-161, 5-185, 6-195, 7-221, 8-225, 9-229

	O	M	R	W
Waqar	14.1	0	52	3
Watkin	9	1	35	0
Thomas	7	1	23	0
Croft	18	4	54	3
Cosker	25	4	64	4

SIX

Rainy Days

Glamorgan v Hampshire
Sophia Gardens, 21–24 May 1997
Britannic Assurance County Championship

		P	Pts
1.	GLOUCESTERSHIRE	3	56
2.	GLAMORGAN	3	43
3.	LEICESTERSHIRE	3	40
4.	NOTTINGHAMSHIRE	3	34
5.	MIDDLESEX	3	31
6.	SOMERSET	3	30
7.	ESSEX	2	29
8.	DURHAM	3	24
9.	SUSSEX	3	24
10.	WARWICKSHIRE	2	23
11.	DERBYSHIRE	3	19
12.	WORCESTERSHIRE	2	17
13.	SURREY	3	17
14.	HAMPSHIRE	3	16
15.	NORTHAMPTONSHIRE	2	16
16.	KENT	2	13
17.	YORKSHIRE	2	13
18.	LANCASHIRE	2	13

I was pleased with the way we had come through the first three
games in the championship against three counties who would, I

expected, be in the top six at the end of the season. I was concerned, as we all were, about the amount of time we were losing to the weather. All three of our championship fixtures had been affected to some extent. Fortunately for us, all the other counties were suffering and no one had managed to open up a significant lead in the table. Only Gloucestershire had won more than one match and we felt we were a better side than they were, though Shaun Young, another Australian, seemed to be a good signing.

We knew it was important to win games in the time available in what was looking increasingly like a wet summer. It was clear that we had to score runs quickly and take every chance offered in the field.

Hampshire arrived at Sophia Gardens with their usual mix of familiar faces and new names. Matthew Hayden, yet another Australian, had promised to make a mountain of runs in the championship after being left out of the Australian Ashes tour. He had not enjoyed a hugely successful start to his season, but he oozed class as he hit us for 57. I have always thought he was a fine player. On the 1993 tour, he made over a thousand first-class runs but did not play in a single Test – he could not break into that so-accomplished top six of Taylor, Slater, Boon, the Waughs and Border. The Australians usually reward form but, on that tour, he had a mammoth task to earn a place.

Scoring over a thousand runs on tour in England and not playing in a Test is unique. Bob Cowper scored a thousand on Bobby Simpson's tour in 1964 but played only one Test innings and that was because of an injury to Norman O'Neill. In the future, though, we might see more batsmen over here hitting a thousand and not winning a cap because their system has done such a great job in producing so many extremely talented batsmen: Ponting, Langer, Martyn, Elliott, Bevan, Blewett and Slater plus those who have been in county cricket like the Laws, Lehmann and Young.

Because the Australian club cricket constitution is aimed at producing players for Australia, the clubs are not parochial: they want success for the greater good. In Australia they have em-braced the concept of 'one game'. If any player shows potential in club cricket in Australia, he is encouraged to go further, to aim for the top. Over here, there is a split in the game between the professional county clubs and the rest. There are two games in this country, the professional and the recreational, whereas the Australians have a seamless progression through to their Test side. We have more of a watershed; it is a huge leap from club cricket to first-class, let alone Test level. The Australian system enables an ambitious and talented player to make his way through the grades and perform against players of equivalent standard right the way through. Here we have a club system that might have players aged 15 and 65 playing in the same game and both scoring hundreds. It is a game which has its attractions and its charm but it is not the type of game they are playing in South Africa and Australia. Our best players in club cricket should be tested each week and the concept of premier leagues is designed to achieve that and improve general standards. There is no intention of removing the social and recreational game from the playing-fields of the UK and it is undoubtedly asking a lot of clubs to change their traditional fixture lists; but the social game will still flourish, while a platform for the ambitious players of potential will hopefully close the gap between county and club cricket.

Robert Croft missed the Hampshire match. He was away with England contesting the Texaco one-day series – successfully too. The game looked in good shape after the whitewash of the Australians. At Cardiff, though, we had problems with Hayden, and then inevitably with Kevan James and Robin Smith. They seem to enjoy playing against us and this game was no exception: James 85, Smith 94. With Dean Cosker solely responsible in the spin department, he continued his education, eventually removing James and Smith by bowling them both.

Robin Smith is still a fine player at 33. He retains all his trademark shots, especially square of the wicket, but after 62 Tests, his England days appear to be over. The England selectors, Messrs Graveney, Gooch and Gatting, made it clear at the start of the season that youth would be given a chance. Quite right too. I am a firm believer in the theory that 'If they are good enough they are old enough', but the operative word is 'good'. Robin is as good as they come, as his Test average of over 43 demonstrates. It was on the 1990 tour of Australia that I became convinced that the best players practise the hardest. In my short time on that tour, I tried to follow Robin's example and we spent hours together in the nets throwing down to each other and generally working on improving our game.

I lost count of the number of times that I have arrived in the carpark at Southampton for a county match and, on climbing out of the car, have heard the crack of bat on ball. No matter how early I arrived, Robin always beat me to it, often with his father to load the bowling machine. There is no more dedicated player in the country than R.A. Smith.

There was more rain to disrupt the match with Hampshire. We were left 310 to win and looked well placed at 279 for five until Hampshire's captain John Stephenson opted to stop us winning rather than pushing for victory himself and posted his fielders around the boundary. A more enterprising approach might have paid off for him; at the close we were eight down and with a little more carrot would have given it some more stick, which could easily have been to Hampshire's advantage. John was only in his second year of captaincy and skippering any side is not easy. Gauging declarations, when to settle for a draw or keep going for the win, are all tricky decisions to make, especially when, whatever is decided, there will always be one member of the side who thinks he knows better (with hindsight, of course). That is why Duncan Fletcher's idea of having the team of three 'senior managers' to back up the captain and manager worked so well. Every player who had an opinion was encouraged to voice it and, as a result, nobody felt excluded.

Taking only four points from the Hampshire game did not help us much, especially as Kent, Yorkshire and Warwickshire all won. Notts also managed to pull off their second win of the season and moved into second place behind Gloucestershire. I was delighted for their captain Paul Johnson, an old friend of mine who came on the 'A' tour to the West Indies in 1992. I was amazed when Peter Roebuck wrote that Notts were 'unworthy of first-class status'. Coming from Somerset, he, of all people, should know that the comparative strengths of county sides tend to be cyclical. Notts have a big grant from the lottery to spend on a cricket centre that should enable a few more youngsters to benefit from some top professional coaching in the east Midlands.

During the Hampshire game, I discovered that several Glamorgan players were fans of daytime TV – including me! Darren Thomas, unlikely as it may seem, enjoyed *Can't Cook Won't Cook* while I loved *Through the Keyhole*. I am fascinated by other people's houses, including those of the physio Dean Conway who seems to own half the properties in Cardiff – a latter-day Rigsby plus ten stone.

Sophia Gardens is a pleasant place to be when the sun shines, but in the rain it takes on another aspect. It becomes obvious just how limited the facilities are. The dressing-rooms have improved since the days when a wall divided the smokers from the non-smokers and senior pros from the juniors. Now the wall has gone and there is a carpet over the concrete floor. Even so, it quickly becomes cluttered with kit, benefit prizes, old bats, autograph books and quietly decomposing socks and sandwiches a week old. Another room for players to relax in would be useful. The members too would appreciate somewhere more comfortable to shelter and pick their World XIs to play Mars.

'Er, excuse me, but you've left out Hobbs and Hutton.'

'Can't get 'em in, bach, not ahead of James and Morris!'

With the award of a £3.2 million lottery grant, Glamorgan could now see their plans to redevelop Sophia Gardens through to fruition. The Welsh public deserve a cricket arena that is capable of staging one-day internationals at least, and should the idea of holding one-day county semi-finals on neutral venues be taken up, Cardiff would be in the running.

If there is a downside, it would be that the bulk (and maybe all) of Glamorgan's first XI games would be played there and the days of 'out grounds' in Wales – Abergavenny, Colwyn Bay, Neath, Pontypridd, and Swansea – could be numbered.

Playing on smaller, prettier, but less well-appointed grounds is a romantic ideal. First-class cricket should be played on grounds with the best facilities and we will have to find other ways of spreading the cricketing gospel than visiting a series of club grounds around the county, or in Glamorgan's case, Wales.

It is often said that Glamorgan is no ordinary county, but a team of that name representing Wales. Robert Croft certainly feels that and Viv Richards and Waqar Younis sensed something of the national pride coming through when they signed up. 'Glamorgan is different to every other county,' Waqar told us during one rain delay at Cardiff. 'It's more like playing for a country than a county, it's a completely different feeling.' He was glad to have joined us. We were overjoyed he did.

Being 'Wales' rather than 'Glamorgan' gives a major obligation to take cricket to the people of Wales, from Haverfordwest to Holyhead, but few grounds could cope with a four-day championship match and not very many more with a Sunday League game. The best way is to create a facility that will be a cricket centre for everyone, with top-class spectator accommodation in a pleasant environment.

Hampshire 1st innings

White	c	James	b	Waqar	6
Hayden			lbw	Watkin	57
James			b	Cosker	85
Smith			b	Cosker	94
Kendall		not out			24
Stephenson		not out			25
Extras					18
Total: 4 wkts dec 88.3 overs					309

DNB: Aymes, Udal, Bovill, Milburn, Connor
Fall: 1-20, 2-100, 3-244, 4-259

	O	M	R	W
Waqar	16	5	39	1
Watkin	24	2	70	1
Thomas	12	0	52	0
Cosker	20	1	61	2
Dale	6.1	2	10	0
Butcher	5	2	16	0
Maynard	3.5	0	30	0
Cottey	1.3	0	17	0

Glamorgan 1st innings forfeited
Hampshire 2nd innings forfeited

Glamorgan 2nd innings

James	c	Aymes	b	Bovill	76
Morris	c	Aymes	b	Stephenson	21
Dale	c	Aymes	b	Bovill	1
Maynard	c	White	b	Bovill	34
Cottey			b	James	34
Butcher			b	Stephenson	58
Shaw			b	Connor	35
Thomas		not out			2
Waqar		run out			1
Watkin		not out			0
Extras					25
Total: 8 wickets 77.5 overs					287

DNB: Cosker

Fall: 1-39, 2-44, 3-100, 4-169, 5-190, 6-279, 7-285, 8-286

	O	M	R	W
Connor	21.5	4	58	1
Milburn	11	1	47	0
Udal	13	4	31	0
Stephenson	12	0	55	2
Bovill	17	3	65	3
James	3	0	20	1

SEVEN

Thanks but no Cigar

Glamorgan v Durham
Sophia Gardens, 29–31 May, 2 June 1997
Britannic Assurance County Championship

		P	Pts
1.	GLOUCESTERSHIRE	4	65
2.	NOTTINGHAMSHIRE	4	54
3.	LEICESTERSHIRE	4	50
4.	GLAMORGAN	4	47
5.	WARWICKSHIRE	3	43
6.	SUSSEX	4	40
7.	ESSEX	3	39
8.	MIDDLESEX	3	36
9.	SOMERSET	4	35
10.	KENT	3	34
11.	YORKSHIRE	3	34
12.	WORCESTERSHIRE	3	33
13.	DURHAM	4	29
14.	DERBYSHIRE	4	26
15.	SURREY	4	26
16.	NORTHAMPTONSHIRE	3	23
17.	HAMPSHIRE	4	20
18.	LANCASHIRE	3	19

At the start of the season, chatting with Duncan Fletcher, we had studied the fixture list and identified several 'must win' games.

These were the matches against counties who were unlikely to challenge for the championship and against whom we expected to pick up, as near as possible, maximum points. The fact that we expected the other title challengers to do the same only emphasised the need to ensure we did not slip up and fall behind in the chase. The beauty of the list that we defined was that all of the 'must wins' were at home – against Hampshire, Durham, Sussex, Gloucestershire and Nottinghamshire.

By the end of May, Gloucestershire were surprising us and Notts were probably even surprising themselves by being in second place. The miserable four points we picked up against Hampshire left us behind on our target from the 'musts', so Durham at Sophia Gardens took on added significance.

At the end of the first day we were 433 for 3. In four-day cricket, whoever has the runs on the board controls the game, and Steve James and I were determined to lay a decent foundation when we opened against Simon Brown and Mike Foster. We did more than that and were feeling pretty pleased with ourselves at putting on 229 for the first wicket. Only twice had we done better than that for the first wicket – against Gloucestershire in 1996 and against Lancashire at Colwyn Bay in 1992. Throughout, we felt in control, ran well between the wickets and, on a beautiful day, the flat pitch was to our advantage. Steve hit a hundred before lunch while I was concentrating on 'granite defence'.

Steve was out for 153 – a lovely innings, always keeping the scoreboard moving and me too. He called me for two all-run fours. Thank goodness for the pre-season training. I was aiming to be first to 500 first-class runs for the season in the country, but though I had an 18-run start over Steve at the start of play, he beat me to it.

It was a good time to have such a productive partnership. David Graveney was looking on – he was due to meet with his fellow selectors Graham Gooch and Mike Gatting later that week to pick an England side to play Australia in the First Test at Edgbaston. Though the one-day internationals had been a clean sweep for England, there were still expected to be one or two changes in the squad. Steve was certainly batting better than I had ever seen him. He used to rely on scoring heavily backward of square on the off side but he developed the ability to make runs all round the wicket. He has adapted his game and improved steadily since he came down from Cambridge University in 1990. He admitted that his technique was getting better, but modestly put his quick scoring down to Durham bowling in 'nice places'. I always knew when Jamer was feeling confident. If I asked if he was in good form he would reply that the bowlers were bowling the ball onto the middle of his bat. When I asked what a particular bowler was bowling, he would simply say, 'Runs!'

Eventually, I reached my 50th first-class hundred for Glamorgan. It was not as eye-catching as Steve's by any means and, after adding 119 for the second wicket with Adrian Dale, I was caught at cover for 135. It was good to hear that Duncan Fletcher was backing a return for me to the England side: 'If Hugh was a South African he would have won a lockerful of caps by now. England are crying out for a batsman of his calibre.' All I could do was keep scoring runs and hope somebody noticed.

Robert Croft on the other side of the dressing-room was an instant reminder that playing for England inevitably brought its share of criticism – some of it unfair. One journalist had written that his 'belly is recovering its former shape after unduly celebrating his winter achievements'. Robert was at pains to point out to anybody within earshot that he had hardly had time to celebrate as no sooner was he back from the England tour than he was into pre-season training with Glamorgan.

We were looking to bowl Durham out as quickly and cheaply as possible and make them follow on. The pitch was still good and their batting has a more formidable look to it than in the past but our bowlers did a magnificent job. They were 81 for five with most of their batting gone. Lewis, Morris, Speak and Speight all out but not Boon. He stayed around, gave Foster the confidence to play his shots and between them they put on 140 for the sixth wicket. On the third day we finished them off for 345 and they followed on, according to plan. Foster's first innings had some glorious moments but from a strictly impartial point of view John Morris was outstanding throughout his second innings' 149. Nobody else made more than 25. We were going for the kill but he played with a freedom that has not been too apparent during his time with Durham. It took more than 200 overs to dismiss them twice on the lifeless pitch. Waqar did produce some reverse swing later on and Steve Watkin, after a quiet start to the season, matched Waqar's seven wickets in the game. It was hard work, much harder than we had imagined, but we achieved our objective – 24 points. At the end John Morris and I met up outside the dressing-room door, and the sentiments were the same from both sides – 'Well played, keep going.'

In a previous incarnation as Derbyshire's number four, he made 175 against us at Swansea in 1988. He was 24 and looked as though he would play at least 20 times for England. Perhaps in 1988 I did too. Indeed, there were a number of players of our generation who looked as though they had the ability to be successful at the highest level. Players like Fairbrother, Bailey, Jarvis, Rhodes, Such, Rose and Johnson all played together for Young England in the early 1980s but none of them established themselves at Test level. I suppose that, at the time, we were all unlucky that the England batting line-up included such luminaries as Gooch, Gower, Gatting, Lamb and Botham for so many years and our generation seemed to miss out.

It was a touch frustrating seeing Johnny playing so well but, even though we were so desperate to win, I was pleased for him personally. He had gone through a dreadful 1996; then, after spending the winter under the guidance of Graham Gooch, was back approaching his best. Johnny flew down from Newcastle to Stansted every week where he was picked up by Graham, driven to the nets and given the great man's undivided attention for a few hours. It obviously paid dividends.

The amazing aspect of the arrangement is that Johnny was with David Gower on the Tiger Moth episode during the 1990–91 Australian tour. It spelt the end of his England career – at the instigation of the then England captain, Graham Gooch. But Johnny has never been one to bear a grudge.

For the first time in four years we were at the top of the

championship table. For as much as we were surprised about
Nottinghamshire and, to a lesser extent, Gloucestershire, there
were those who thought our climb to the top was the result of
a favourable fixture list, while rain was ruining the chances of
the title favourites. Our championship form over the three
previous seasons did not suggest that we were title material – in
fact, many of the critics labelled us a 'useful one-day side'. A
closer look at the way we had played against the better
opposition, Warwickshire and Kent particularly, gave a strong
indication that we could last the pace. Certainly, one of our
long-distance supporters, Gareth Phillips from Solva, hoped so.
He had backed us for the championship pre-season and had
been quoted odds of 50 to 1!

Being championship leaders was unlikely to go to our heads.
In 1993 we had taken the lead in June only to lose it, crucially,
when Middlesex beat us at Cardiff in the first week of July. We
lost by ten wickets in an astonishing turnaround. (We had made
562 for three declared in our first innings with unbeaten double
centuries for both Viv Richards and Adrian Dale.)

Furthermore, our feet were kept firmly on the ground by
Glamorgan's former players, who held their annual reunion
during the Durham match. I have always listened to their stories
and anecdotes with real pleasure. I enjoyed popping into the
committee room to see them all again.

Don Shepherd was there, of course. Any occasion at
Glamorgan would not be 'official' without Shep. Alan Jones
added the batsman's perspective. All-rounder Peter Walker could
keep the balance if not the peace and there were more recent
Old Boys like Geoff Holmes and John Hopkins, a couple of the
'48 champions, Phil Clift and the organiser of the whole event,
Jim Pleass. Inevitably, there was sadness. Three very notable
names who had been such outstanding members of the Old
Players' Association had recently died: Willie Jones, so close to
being a double international at rugby and cricket, a Glamorgan
left-hander who once hit two double centuries in a fortnight;
Ernie Harris, played both pre- and post-war, a fine club
cricketer with St Fagans and later was on the county
committee; and Wilf Wooller. He was Glamorgan for so long –

captain, secretary, president. We had many discussions and many arguments about players and playing and how to play. It was never dull. He was also, I should imagine, close to being a double international. He played 18 times at centre for Wales. There was more than one occasion when I was captain when Wilf would suddenly appear through the door of a team meeting with an idea, a theory – even once upon a time bursting in with a piece of paper for Robert Croft detailing the field placements for Graham Hick the next time he bowled against him. I would say to him, 'Wilf, who's the bloody captain here?' And we would both end up laughing, because he was, in his own mind, always the captain.

A few years ago, Dick Richardson, the Worcestershire and England batsman, told me of an incident during the Worcester-shire-Glamorgan game at Worcester in 1957. Worcestershire had been caught on a drying pitch and Jim McConnon had taken eight of the nine Worcestershire wickets to fall. He wanted one more for a career best and to set the best analysis for the season. The last pair – Bob Berry and Len Coldwell – were in and everyone in the Glamorgan side was made aware that the last wicket had to be Jim's, even to the extent of bowling wides so as not to get anyone out.

Peter Walker bowled to Berry who dollied a catch back, but Peter, who never dropped catches, deliberately let this one bounce out of hands and it landed on the stumps with Coldwell out of his ground backing up. There was silence for a while. Peter was even in the process of picking up the bails, when a lone voice from cover shouted, 'How's that?' Everybody stared at Willie Jones. 'What's the matter? What have I done?' he asked. The umpire Paul Gibb had no option but to give Len Coldwell 'Run out' and Jim McConnon never did take nine wickets in an innings.

Wilf was furious and ran after Willie, who saw him coming and sprinted off towards the pavilion. He was up the steps and into the lavatory at the back of the dressing-room in no time. Wilf pounded after him and for a full hour hammered on the door, cursing and swearing at Willie and threatening to do all sorts of impossibly painful things to various parts of Willie's anatomy.

Willie's *faux pas* was compounded a fortnight later when Kent's Dave Halfyard bowled Glamorgan out in two hours at Neath by taking nine for 39 – including the unfortunate Willie for a duck.

No Wilf and no Willie around anymore at the Old Players' reunions, sad to say. One tradition will undoubtedly continue: on such occasions there will continue to be instant recall of games where not a false shot was played nor a half-volley was bowled!

There were times when, on the Sunday mornings of the announcement of the England Test side, I would be awake before seven, pacing around nervously, half reading the papers and drinking too much coffee. Having heard the team, I would then slope off to sulk in the shower.

Three times I was delighted to hear my name solemnly read out in that alphabetical list. Since 1993, though, listening to the team has been more of an academic exercise, idle curiosity with hopes of a place for Croft, Maynard or Watkin.

On the Sunday of the Durham game the phone rang. Debbi answered it. Holding her hand over the mouthpiece, she whispered, 'It's David Graveney.' For a moment, thoughts of opening again for England flashed through my mind. They were immediately dispelled when David began: 'This isn't the call you've been waiting for.' It was disappointing but the knowledge that I was even in the frame after such a long time out of contention was some compensation. Grav explained that the selectors had decided to stick with the policy that had proved successful in the one-day internationals and promote the young players. Mark Butcher was in for his first cap. It was good to know that the chairman was using man–management skills; he did not have to explain the selectors' decisions to me.

I had another cup of coffee and sloped off to sulk in the shower.

Glamorgan 1st innings

James			c&b	Boiling	153
Morris	c	Morris	b	Collingwood	135
Dale			lbw	Walker	73
Maynard		not out			134
Cottey	c	Collingwood	b	Brown	15
Croft	c	Collingwood	b	Foster	29
Shaw			lbw	Cox	33
Waqar	c	Collingwood	b	Cox	7
Thomas	c	Boon	b	Cox	0
Extras					18
Total: 8 wkts dec 140.3 overs					597

DNB: Watkin Cosker

Fall: 1-229, 2-348, 3-408, 5-509, 6-584, 7-594, 8-597

	O	M	R	W
Brown	33	4	113	1
Foster	22	4	122	1
Walker	26	4	112	1
Boiling	33	5	117	1
Collingwood	11	1	51	1
Cox	15.3	2	72	3

Durham 1st innings

Lewis	c	Maynard	b	Watkin	21
Collingwood	c	Croft	b	Waqar	17
Morris			b	Watkin	20
Speak	c	Shaw	b	Waqar	10
Boon			b	Waqar	66
Speight			b	Thomas	5
Foster			lbw	Croft	129
Cox			b	Thomas	24
Boiling		not out			10
Brown			c&b	Watkin	1
Walker			b	Watkin	16
Extras					26
Total: all out 110.2 overs					345

Fall: 1-23, 2-58, 3-59, 4-76, 5-81, 6-221, 7-259, 8-328, 9-329

	O	M	R	W
Waqar	22	4	98	3
Watkin	28.2	10	73	4
Thomas	20	7	59	2
Croft	25	8	51	1
Cosker	12	4	41	0
Dale	3	2	5	0

Durham 2nd innings

Lewis			lbw	Watkin	5
Collingwood			lbw	Waqar	1
Morris	c	Cottey	b	Waqar	149
Speak			b	Thomas	25
Boon			lbw	Waqar	15
Boiling	c	Cottey	b	Croft	4
Speight			b	Waqar	1
Cox	c	Maynard	b	Watkin	0
Brown	c	Cottey	b	Croft	5
Walker		not out			10
Extras:					18
Total: all out 93 overs					244

Fall: 1-5, 2-13, 3-97, 4-141, 5-152, 6-165, 7-193, 8-193, 9-200

	O	M	R	W
Waqar	20	7	56	4
Watkin	18	7	31	3
Croft	33	10	81	2
Thomas	9	1	28	1
Dale	5	2	10	0
Cosker	8	2	26	0

EIGHT

Going Underground

Glamorgan v Middlesex
Sophia Gardens, 12-14 June 1997
Britannic Assurance County Championship

		P	Pts
1.	GLOUCESTERSHIRE	5	86
2.	KENT	5	81
3.	NOTTINGHAMSHIRE	6	80
4.	GLAMORGAN	5	71
5.	MIDDLESEX	5	71
6.	LEICESTERSHIRE	6	70
7.	ESSEX	5	68
8.	SOMERSET	6	65
9.	YORKSHIRE	6	61
10.	WARWICKSHIRE	5	58
11.	HAMPSHIRE	5	55
12.	DURHAM	6	43
13.	WORCESTERSHIRE	4	43
14.	SUSSEX	4	41
15.	LANCASHIRE	5	33
16.	SURREY	5	32
17.	DERBYSHIRE	5	32
18.	NORTHAMPTONSHIRE	5	31

A break from the county championship to play Oxford University in The Parks was, for me, blessed relief. A week off.

After a couple of days I was thinking I might have preferred facing Walsh and Ambrose in the dark rather than tackling the succession of jobs around the house that had been put off until I 'had a minute'. But it was very pleasant to be able to play with the twins without the knowledge that such precious moments would be cut short because I had to pack up and drive off up the motorway for another five days away from home.

Mike Powell, 20 years old from Abergavenny, had been given his chance in the first XI after scoring a cluster of centuries for the second team, including two unbeaten hundreds to win the match with Kent against the clock at Pontardulais. It was a performance that had impressed coach John Derrick and Kevin Lyons, who was umpiring. He scored his runs against no ordinary second-XI attack – Kent had included Nick Preston and Ed Stanford, both of whom had played in the county championship, and Dr Julian Thompson, famous as the man who dismissed Brian Lara for a pair in 1995 and whose first three wickets in 1996 were Atherton, Gatting and Gooch.

Powell obviously found the Oxford University bowling to his liking too as he made an unbeaten 200. He became only the third batsman in England since the war to score a double century on his début, the others being Hubert Doggart for Cambridge University against Lancashire in 1948 and David Sales for North-amptonshire against Worcestershire at Kidderminster in 1996.

The previous Glamorgan player to have scored a hundred on his début was Matthew Maynard who made a mightily impressive start to his county career in 1985 when he came in against Yorkshire at Swansea and hammered them for 102 out of 117 in only 87 minutes, reaching his hundred with three succes-sive sixes off Phil Carrick – all three carrying onto the terraces of the rugby ground. (Carrick bowled well in that innings – he took seven for 99.) For Matthew, it was a remarkable entry into first-class cricket and no fluke as he has proved by mounting many similar assaults in the years since. Matthew was only 19 at the time. By contrast, I was well over 20, nearly 21 in fact, when I made my first hundred. Mike Powell was in good company; it was important though that he 'trained on'.

While we were otherwise engaged, our rivals for the

championship had overtaken us. Gloucestershire had beaten Yorkshire at Headingley and Mike Smith had taken ten in a match again. He used to captain Yorkshire Schools so that was a big result for him. There have been some left-arm seamers tried and discarded by England over the years – Ilott, Taylor, Mullally, Brown – but none has stayed the course for more than nine Test matches. Smith was being touted as the next to be called up but if he was to succeed, conditions had to be in his favour, helping the ball to swing.

Kent had moved up to second as they beat Warwickshire and Notts were third after scoring over 300 to beat Northants with a century for Matthew Dowman. Dowman promised so much at 19 when he scored 267 for England Under-19s against the West Indies who included Chanderpaul, Ramnarine and Rawl Lewis, all of whom are now making progress in the Caribbean. Dowman's chances have been restricted by injury but in 1997 he had an opportunity to shine in a Notts side that was not especially strong. With Middlesex drawing level with us on points after a draw with Leicestershire, the match at Cardiff became very important.

Anyone who has been around county cricket for any length of time will be able to tell of strange games, unlikely occurrences and unusual happenings. This game was probably the most bizarre I have ever played in.

We had beaten Middlesex in one-day competitions in recent years, while struggling terribly against them in the championship. Since 1993 we had lost to them successively by ten wickets, 80 runs, eight wickets and nine wickets. In that time Emburey, Gatting, Pooley, Carr and Brown had all hit centuries off our bowlers and Tufnell had taken eight for 29 in one innings, Weekes eight for 39 in another and Emburey six for 89 in a third. With Emburey gone to Northants and Gatting handing over the captaincy to Ramprakash, now was the time we could exact a little revenge.

Our 281 was not a bad total against their bowling attack – Fraser, Hewitt, Johnson and Tufnell, with Croft making a season's best so far of 82. It was fewer than we hoped but still something for us to bowl at.

Jacques Kallis opened for Middlesex. Well known to Duncan Fletcher, since he plays for Western Province, we knew he was an aggressive cricketer who would slaughter any wayward bowling. Not much was off line but he rattled along to 96. He loved Waqar. As fast as Waqar bowled from the Cathedral Road End, the more Kallis relished it. If Waqar pitched up, he was driven straight or through the off side. If it was short, he hooked him square or fine depending on where the fielders were stationed. It was an exhilarating display from a 21-year-old, reminiscent of that other South African, Kevin McKenzie. Middlesex were 237 for three and then fell apart – 319 all out as Watty and Thomas took four wickets each.

At the close of the second day I had a drink with the BBC newsreader Chris Lowe, who is on the Middlesex committee. As we said goodbye, he looked forward to a good day's cricket on the Saturday. 'Oh, I suppose I will be standing quietly at slip all day,' I said. How wrong can you be? By late afternoon, I was at home and thinking of doing a little gardening before supper.

Having bowled Middlesex out, we took the heavy roller. Usually, that is no big deal at Sophia Gardens; the pitch tends be deadened for a while, which gives us a decent opportunity of a good start. Yet, all of a sudden, the ball started to go underground. Within 16 overs we were bowled out for 31. It was incredible. I had never experienced anything like it before.

Usually when seamers are able to keep the ball low, the bounce at a minimum, deliveries either miss everything or batsmen nick balls into their pads. Not on this occasion. Steve James was LBW to Fraser for 2. Then Gus got me in a similar way for 5. We were 11 for four when Robert Croft marched out to join Tony Cottey.

Once in the middle, Crofty let fly to Cotts about the indiscipline of the top order, suggesting that we had been more interested in watching the British Lions on television than in fighting for the cause.

James Hewitt's first ball to Robert shot straight along the ground and trapped him right in front. He arrived back in the dressing-room having missed no more than two minutes of the second half of the Lions match.

It was around this time that the members and the press had started to make noises about the continued absence of Colin

Metson from the team. Adrian Shaw had not had the best of times behind the stumps and he had not yet scored a 50. The Middlesex game only increased the pressure on him. He was out for nought and one and he began to feel even more sensitive about playing at home.

In the dressing-room, there was not even the kind of fatalistic, under-the-blitz type humour that had been apparent when we had collapsed, not quite so dramatically, in the past. We had put our title ambitions on the line against one of the stronger counties and had been found seriously wanting. We were badly shaken by the manner of the defeat and it could have been the end of our challenge.

That it was not the end is due in large part to Duncan Fletcher. I doubt if he could believe what had happened either, but he managed to convince us all that it was a complete fluke. The management team had a job to do now. We told each other that we had not become poor players overnight, that we had to back our ability and give each other encouragement. The most important thing was not to panic and, as Duncan said, 'Make sure we win the next game.'

It was then that the records started to be quoted at us – the lowest score ever against Middlesex in the county championship. That was a surprise. It meant that even when Middlesex had an all-star attack – Daniel, Fraser, Edmonds, Emburey etc and we were not that hot – we had still not been bowled out for 31. It was our lowest total for 26 years, so even some of Glamorgan's weakest teams had not suffered as we did.

We did not need to be told that it was a poor performance. There were extenuating circumstances, but no first-class side should be out in 16 overs in a first-class game, well as James Hewitt and Gus Fraser bowled. Yet of course the letters came in, some of them abusive. We had 'bottled it', we were not 'championship material', how there were 'better players in the local leagues' – and these were from our own supporters! I doubt if there is anyone more fickle than a cricket fan, for the sole reason that they are so completely involved in the game. If we lose, they are let down. One letter from a Mr Jones of Dolgellau in Merionethshire was quickly and justifiably binned. He wrote of the season being over for us, how there was no hope of winning anything with the team that we had and that it had been a mistake to invest so much in 'washed-up Waqar'. How I wish that I had kept the letter, or at least the man's address. I would love to hear his comments now.

Even some members of the committee could not understand that it was a time for encouragement and support, not to be clucking into their pints at the bar, shaking their heads and muttering about the team needing more backbone and 'what happened to the famous batting line-up?'

Criticism should be justified and it was just not the right time for all our previous efforts to be disregarded. The team pulled together, convinced by Duncan and Matthew that the session against Middlesex was an aberration. It was certainly that. Our worst of the season, in hindsight, but it was not time for backsides to be kicked, for wholesale changes to be made or for everyone to let off steam. We had to regroup, keep to the same routine and remain optimistic.

It was a blow for Steve James who had been going so well. Three and two were not the scores to set before an England selector at first hand, but Mike Gatting had been around cricket for long enough to know that it was impossible to judge a player on one match. Beneath that gung-ho, up-and-at-'em! exterior, there is an astute cricketing brain. He did a great job as the captain of Middlesex, when it could all so easily have fallen apart after the retirement of Mike Brearley.

He is such a brilliant character to have around the game — knowledgeable, humorous, always ready for a chat and a beer (and lunch, tea and dinner). For many, he will always be remembered for the Shakoor Rana episode in Pakistan. For those of us in the game, he is respected for his competitiveness and his sportsmanlike attitude. Off the field he is gregarious and generous. In 1994 we took a young side up to Lord's for the championship match, including Alistair Dalton, Owen Parkin, Stuart Phelps and Adrian Shaw — all playing in their first match at the headquarters of cricket. At the end of the first day, they went to Crocker's, the pub around the corner from the ground. Gatt did not know a single one of them, but he was first to go across to their group, introduce himself and buy them all a drink.

The following evening, he discovered that I had a benefit dinner at Enfield – his part of the world. He could not resist dropping in, entertaining everyone with a question-and-answer session and he stayed late into the evening. The next morning, my benefit committee chairman Richard Harris, who had stayed in the Lord's flat of ground superintendent Gareth Williams, was woken by the sound of bat on ball coming from the Nursery End. It was Gatt, of course.

The Saturday evening of the Middlesex disaster, I stared at the lawn growing and tried to remember the last time I had been in a side that had been bowled out for 31. The nearest was probably 1988 when Lancashire shot us out at Swansea for 47. Then, on a pitch that was taking spin, Jack Simmons and Ian Folley bowled us out in an hour and a half. That was a dismal day too.

From upstairs came the sounds of Bethan and Emily splashing happily in the bath. As always, they brought me back to reality.

Glamorgan 1st innings

James	c	Brown	b	Fraser	3
Morris	c	Kallis	b	Hewitt	16
Dale	c	Kallis	b	Fraser	0
Maynard	c	Brown	b	Hewitt	59
Cottey	c	Weekes	b	Johnson	19
Croft	c	Brown	b	Fraser	82
Butcher	c	Weekes	b	Shaw	21
Shaw			b	Fraser	0
Waqar	c	Fraser	b	Tufnell	26
Thomas		not out			11
Watkin	c	Brown	b	Johnson	4
Extras					40
Total: all out 92 overs					281

Fall: 1-10, 2-26, 3-26, 4-64, 5-148, 6-216, 7-217, 8-240, 9-269

	O	M	R	W
Fraser	24	4	68	4
Hewitt	23	3	88	3
Kallis	2	2	0	0
Johnson	20	5	55	2
Tufnell	14	4	31	1
Dutch	9	2	13	0

Middlesex 1st innings

Weekes	c	Thomas	b	Watkin	3
Kallis	c	Maynard	b	Watkin	96
Ramprakash	c	Shaw	b	Watkin	63
Gatting	c	Shaw	b	Thomas	28
Pooley			lbw	Croft	40
Fraser	c	Shaw	b	Watkin	8
Brown			lbw	Thomas	12
Dutch	c	Shaw	b	Thomas	4
Johnson	c	Maynard	b	Waqar	6
Hewitt		not out			15
Tufnell			b	Thomas	21
Extras					23
Total: all out 105.2 overs					319

Fall: 1-5, 2-165, 3-172, 4-237, 5-243, 6-259, 7-265, 8-272, 9-278

	O	M	R	W
Waqar	22	2	89	1
Watkin	27	12	43	4
Thomas	21.2	5	52	4
Croft	27	3	90	1
Butcher	5	1	21	0
Dale	3	1	9	0

Glamorgan 2nd inngs

James			lbw	Fraser	2
Morris			lbw	Fraser	5
Dale			c&b	Hewitt	2
Maynard			lbw	Fraser	0
Cottey			lbw	Hewitt	12
Croft			lbw	Hewitt	0
Butcher			b	Hewitt	0
Shaw	c	Gatting	b	Hewitt	1
Waqar			lbw	Fraser	2
Thomas		not out			0
Watkin	c	Brown	b	Hewitt	0
Extras					0
Total: all out 16 overs					31

Fall: 1-2, 2-7, 3-7, 4-11, 5-11, 6-11, 7-21, 8-24, 9-24

	O	M	R	W
Fraser	8	2	17	4
Hewitt	8	4	14	6

NINE

Back with a Bang

Lancashire v Glamorgan
Aigburth, 18–21 June 1997
Britannic Assurance County Championship

		P	Pts
1.	KENT	6	105
2.	MIDDLESEX	6	94
3.	ESSEX	6	92
4.	GLOUCESTERSHIRE	6	91
5.	NOTTINGHAMSHIRE	6	80
6.	GLAMORGAN	6	77
7.	HAMPSHIRE	7	76
8.	YORKSHIRE	6	71
9.	LEICESTERSHIRE	6	70
10.	SOMERSET	6	69
11.	WARWICKSHIRE	6	68
12.	WORCESTERSHIRE	5	65
13.	SUSSEX	6	45
14.	SURREY	6	43
15.	DURHAM	6	43
16.	DERBYSHIRE	6	40
17.	LANCASHIRE	6	39
18.	NORTHAMPTONSHIRE	5	31

On the road again, M4, M5, M6, M62 to Liverpool. The weather forecast was for rain and more rain, not what we wanted when

we were desperate to remove the shadow of that Saturday afternoon against Middlesex. The good news was that Lancashire had
half their first-choice side missing, all Test players too – Atherton,
Gallian, Crawley, Wasim and Watkinson.

Driving up, Watty and I were trying to decide when we had
last played at Liverpool. Was it 1990 or 1991? I remembered that
Alan Butcher had scored two centuries in the match.

'Probably 1990 then.'

'Must have been.'

'Shastri scored a hundred same match.'

'Couldn't have been 1990 then.'

'Why not?'

'Viv played in 1990. Ravi in 1991 when Viv was on tour with
the West Indies.'

'Know-all.'

So monotonous journeys fly past with such scintillating
conversation. We really do talk about anything and everything,
from politics to players' form, and we used to have a £1 bet on
the identity of the umpires who would be standing in the forth-
coming match. In the days when I was captain I won on a
regular basis as Watty had no idea that the umpires had been
decided some weeks in advance and club captains were aware of
who had been allocated. When I was not captain, we evened up
a little, but not much.

Incidentally, it rained during that match in 1991, but not half
as much as it did in 1997.

On the first day, play was called off with us 173 for one and
Steve James was 99 not out. I was the 'one'. Caught at the wicket
off 'Bully' Austin for 24. He is a tremendous all-round cricketer,
a great trier and, as a bowler, exploits conditions to his advantage,
rarely bowling a loose ball and hits the bat hard. He is one of
those bowlers that touring teams hate facing when there is some
movement in the air or off the pitch. Nobody else is too keen
either.

Turning up at a ground first thing in the morning and
realising that there is little prospect of play is a depressing
exercise. At Liverpool we lost two days completely. As they only
play one first-class fixture at Aigburth a season, the local cricket

fans were not exactly well treated by the weather, but it gave our team the chance to indulge in a few time-honoured pastimes. Allocating nicknames is one juvenile activity – the not very original 'Old Spice' was one of the first to be given, hardly appropriately. 'Speedy Spice' for Waqar, because he not only bowls quickly but also had a sponsored Jaguar XJ Sport to drive around the country in. Skinny, Skeleton, Fat, Pixie and Drunken were given to the other Glamorgan 'Spice Boys'. Last year, Christian names were altered to the Welsh equivalents – hence Shadwel, Dyfig, Meurig and Teifion.

During the rain breaks there are various activities to occupy the team. I was often to be found with the card-sharps, Maynard, Cottey and Dale. Failing that, I'd attempt crosswords like James, though not half as successfully. Thomas, Butcher, Cosker were the ace devisers of various forms of dressing-room cricket. Shaw spent most of his spare time waxing lyrical on any and every subject (eventually to himself) and Croft, when he was not interrupting everyone else's ways of keeping amused, thankfully fell asleep.

Liverpool gave Duncan Fletcher and me a chance to visit Anfield. Quite why a Cowbridge-born rugby-playing cricketer should form such an attachment to Liverpool FC is inexplicable. It could have been something to do with the number of Manchester United fans who proliferated in our neighbourhood in the early 1970s when I wanted to be different to the rest of the crowd. It is more likely that the roots of my affection started when the great John Toshack was transferred to Liverpool from Cardiff at the end of 1970 at a time when United were going downhill. I certainly tended to support successful Welsh sports-people in any and every team, and Liverpool were the team of the 1970s.

Nowadays it is so obvious that youngsters support success. In the late 1960s we would quote 'Jones, Davis, Majid, Lewis ...' or Carwyn James's Lions: 'JPR, Bevan, Davies, Dawes ...' but kids today want to wear the shirts of their heroes. On my visits to the primary and junior schools of South Wales when I was coaching cricket during the winters, it was quite amazing just how many replica shirts were being worn by the pupils. I would estimate that over 75 per cent would have been in the various colours and styles of Manchester United, whilst another 25 per cent accounted for Liverpool and Newcastle United.

Saturday, unexpectedly, dawned clear if not exactly bright. Lancashire's stand-in captain Neil Fairbrother struck a deal with Matthew Maynard: they were to be left about 65 overs to make 275 to win. Steve James had been on 99 not out for two and a half days – it must be some kind of record – but he rattled along to 152 not out as Lancashire provided ten overs of rubbish for Steve and Daley to collect another 100 runs.

There was some discussion in the dressing-room about the target. I thought it was too easy for them; we had scored 272 in 60 overs on a pitch that was absolutely faultless.

Fourteen overs later we were back in the dressing-room, the proud owners of 18 points from the match which we had managed to win by 221 runs.

Games of forfeit are always games of chance too, usually favouring the side to do the chasing, who are in the best position to negotiate a good deal. Unfortunately for Lancashire, Waqar, having been cooped up for three days, let rip. Nathan Wood and Glenn Chapple both went for ducks and it might easily have been a hat-trick for Waqar as Harvey would have walked for the LBW shout next ball if that had been the done thing. It was the first time we had seen Waqar swinging the ball prodigiously to such good effect. The hat-trick duly arrived when he sent back Chilton, Hegg and Yates and he finished with career-best figures of seven for 25 from seven overs. Great support came from the other end, Watty giving nothing away in his three for 21 from seven overs.

Lancashire had made a few behind-the-hand comments about us being bowled out by Middlesex in 16 overs. Now they had gone down in only 14. It was the comeback we had all hoped for, but thought the rain had put paid to.

The tour of the Anfield Stadium was a fascinating experience. Compared with the facilities available for Premier Division footballers, ours in cricket seem very primitive. The stadium was in the process of being refurbished during our visit, and even the famous trophy-room was receiving a major refit. The estimated cost was a few hundred thousand pounds. We could have built virtually a whole new pavilion for the same price.

As we wandered around there was no denying that there was a certain aura about the place. The pride and the passion for football could be sensed everywhere, even in a ground empty apart from workmen, builders and painters. Running out onto the pitch in front of a packed house must be an awesome experience.

The Balconiers enjoyed their trip to Liverpool though they missed the whole point of the exercise by not seeing a ball bowled. They arrived for the second day and for 48 hours watched the rain tipping down. With another day of rain forecast for the Saturday, they decided they might as well shuttle off to Manchester for a tour of the Granada TV studios, especially *Coronation Street*. So they missed the hectic events of the last day. They are a solid band of Glamorgan supporters, mainly from the west of Wales – well, of Cardiff, anyway – who follow the team to virtually every away match. It is very much a social club. Sampling the local restaurants and pubs is very high on the list of priorities, one behind the cricket. Other activities do get a look in, though. One of the Balconiers is a mad keen Country and Western fan who, after a day's play at Lord's, jumped into a cab to go to a C&W concert. The taxi hurtled off down a side street and stopped. The driver came round into the back seat and informed the querulous Balconier that he urgently required the kiss of life. For every subsequent journey the member took in London, he went by bus and tube.

At present there are about 500 members of the Balconiers. Not only do they supply valuable vocal support at matches, they also make annual presentations to their choice of Player of the Year, Most Improved Player of the Year, Second XI Player of the Year, and contribute funds to the club itself.

Darren Thomas had the task of organising the venue for the weekly team meal – a recipe for disaster if ever there was one. During a pre-season tour of Zimbabwe a couple of years ago, the Glamorgan team were invited to a hog roast in Owe Owe, a small town in the middle of the country. Darren typically found his way to the front of the queue and helped himself to a huge slice of meat from the pig that was being roasted. It did not take long for him to clear his plate and, being a growing lad, he still felt a little peckish. He looked up to see his mate Gary Butcher at the head of the queue and about to carve some meat for himself. So Darren shouted across: 'Hey, Butch, cut some more beef off that pig for me, please!'

We were all pleasantly surprised when it appeared that the team meal was not about to be the chaotic occasion we had all feared.

'Where are we going?' I asked Darren.

'The Maissez-vous,' he replied. 'It's a little place the hotel porter told me about. I think it's a French bistro or something.'

It turned out to be an 'or something', a Beefeater steak bar, in fact, called The Pier that had a great 'Mersey view'.

Harvey was philosophical after our victory. He was experienced enough and realistic enough to know that a great bowler had bowled out of his skin. Harv has been a top-class player over the years, one of my closest mates on the county circuit. We first played together in 1981 for England Schools and have since shared the highs and lows of touring and the competition of county cricket.

He is never shy of a word and came out with an endless stream of sarcastic comments while I was batting. Indeed, during the game at Aigburth, I missed out with the bat much to the pleasure of Harvey as he and Bully Austin teed me up. 'Give him a bouncer, Bully,' Harvey called from slip.

Bully, walking back, turned and said, 'Shall I?'

'Tell you what,' said Harvey, 'we'll put a man back this ball and make sure you bounce him.'

Sure enough the man went back to deep square leg.

'No double bluffing now,' shouted Harvey as Bully reached his mark. I was taking guard, thinking, 'Will he or won't he?' It was the slowest pitch of the season so I thought he probably wouldn't, but then he might. Shall I hook or leave it?

It was a situation I had been in a thousand times during my career, but, like a good captain, Harvey had genuinely put me in two minds.

In came Bully and, inevitably, he dropped it short. I went for the hook and gloved a catch to the keeper. I had fallen for one of the oldest tricks in the book. And, for the next three days at Aigburth, Harvey did not let me forget it.

Glamorgan 1st innings

James		not out			152
Morris	c	Hegg	b	Austin	24
Dale		not out			78
Extras					18
Total 1 wkt dec 60.1 overs					272

DNB: Maynard, Cottey, Butcher, Shaw, Waqar, Thomas, Cosker, Watkin

Fall: 1-62

	O	M	R	W
Martin	14	3	32	0
Chapple	12	2	31	0
Austin	15	7	41	1
Keedy	5	1	26	0
Chilton	4	0	23	0
Yates	1	0	8	0
Lloyd	5	0	59	0
Wood	4.1	0	38	0

Lancashire 1st innings forfeited
Glamorgan 2nd innings forfeited

Lancashire 2nd innings

Wood			lbw	Waqar	0
Titchard			lbw	Waqar	5
Chapple			b	Waqar	0
Fairbrother			b	Watkin	5
Lloyd	c	Shaw	b	Waqar	7
Chilton	c	Shaw	b	Waqar	9
Austin		not out			17
Hegg	c	Shaw	b	Waqar	0
Yates			b	Waqar	0
Martin			lbw	Watkin	1
Keedy	c	Waqar	b	Watkin	0
Extras					7
Total: all out 14 overs					51

Fall: 1-4, 2-4, 3-13, 4-17, 5-27, 6-38, 7-50, 8-50, 9-51

	O	M	R	W
Waqar	7	1	25	7
Watkin	7	3	21	3

GLAMORGAN IN THE 1997 NAT WEST TROPHY ROUND ONE

24.6.97   beat Bedfordshire at Cardiff by seven wickets
            Bedfordshire 179 for six (60 overs)
            Glamorgan 182 for three (30.2 overs)

This was a straightforward win for us with Robert Croft named the Man of the Match for his 64 and bowling 12 overs for 14 runs and one wicket.

There is a case for arguing that these matches against Minor Counties should be played on the Minor County grounds. It would certainly improve the atmosphere and give more chance of a surprise result. The professionals, however, will always prefer to play on the best wickets with the most comfortable pavilions, closest to home!

TEN

Sussex by the Sea

Glamorgan v Sussex
St Helen's, 26–30 June 1997
Britannic Assurance County Championship

		P	Pts
1.	MIDDLESEX	7	115
2.	KENT	7	109
3.	GLOUCESTERSHIRE	7	95
4.	GLAMORGAN	7	95
5.	ESSEX	6	92
6.	NOTTINGHAMSHIRE	7	87
7.	HAMPSHIRE	8	83
8.	LEICESTERSHIRE	7	81
9.	YORKSHIRE	7	81
10.	SOMERSET	8	76
11.	WORCESTERSHIRE	6	72
12.	WARWICKSHIRE	6	68
13.	DURHAM	7	65
14.	SUSSEX	7	53
15.	SURREY	7	50
16.	DERBYSHIRE	7	48
17.	LANCASHIRE	7	39
18.	NORTHAMPTONSHIRE	6	36

The win at Aigburth was exactly what was required after the
Middlesex débâcle. If we had lost against Lancashire or been

completely rained off, we would have had time to dwell on the Middlesex beating and that would have been very unhealthy. Duncan Fletcher would probably have noticed the signs, however, and designed some method of keeping us amused, fit and on course for the next 'must win' game, Sussex at Swansea.

There is less first-class cricket at Swansea these days and the prospect of very little in the future. The increasing importance of Sophia Gardens, plus rugby eating into the cricket season and the much publicised decision by the Swansea council not to provide a £10,000 guarantee to the county club means that its days as a first-class venue are now limited. In 1997 we played only twice at Swansea, against Sussex and Gloucestershire. In the early part of my career I enjoyed playing at St Helen's. Maybe it was the rugby atmosphere, the proximity of the sea and the ozone in the air. It was certainly something to do with the pitches, tended with loving care by George Clements, and the crowd, friendly and knowledgeable and pleased to see us 'out west'.

We never knew what kind of pitch we might play on at Swansea in latter days. More heavy rain during the week leading up to the Sussex game meant that the wicket was inevitably damp and produced considerable movement for the seamers.

James Kirtley took six wickets as we struggled to put together a decent total. Kirtley, at 22, looks a good prospect. He is the man who took seven wickets in the match for Mashonaland against England during the winter. Whatever Sussex could achieve on that pitch we knew that, with our balanced attack, we could do better. In fact, their first innings was all over inside 23 overs, Waqar bowling unchanged took eight for 17 (another career-best) from 11.5 overs. Everyone knows of Waqar's ability to swing the old ball – the infamous 'reverse swing' – but during the winter in Australia he developed the out-swinger with the new ball and in the two games at Liverpool and Swansea he used it to devastating effect. His combined figures:18.5-5-42-15!

Few of us knew much about Waqar when he joined us, having only experienced being on the receiving end of the Sultan of Swing. It was a real pleasure to see him fitting in so well in the dressing-room. There is no false image there. He is a real team man with a tremendous desire to win. It was noticeable, though, that he is still a young man – only 27 – and at times appears younger because he has a shyness and a curious awkwardness about him in company sometimes. He was a most popular recruit, though, even having a local balti restaurant named after him in Cardiff. He was also given an honorary degree – presumably not by one of those university science departments who spend so much time trying to prove that cricket balls cannot swing.

Sussex were all out for 54 in their first innings and then, needing 302 to win, were rattled out in under 33 overs for 67. Darren Thomas was the most effective bowler this time with five wickets. The highest score in the game was Steve James's 82 not out in our second innings. Matthew Maynard made 61. Between them they scored more than the whole of the Sussex XI in two combined innings. It was not all plain sailing for Glamorgan, though. This kind of game is not the one to play in when your batting is not in its best shape. Tony Cottey made a pair, Adrian Dale nought and six, Darren Thomas a pair, and I was little better with 11 and three.

Sussex are in the doldrums. Having been there with Glamorgan, I can sympathise with their problems. It is important to have men of experience in vital positions in the team. Sussex, having lost Wells, Speight, Giddins, Salisbury, Law and coach Desmond Haynes for a variety of reasons, have little experience to call on. It is crucial to have professionals in the side who are familiar with all aspects of the game. Essentially, a county side would expect to have its most experienced men opening the batting, with two seniors in the middle order, plus an experienced seamer and a spinner. With those six positions filled, the opportunity is there to bring on five younger players without them having such a high level of expectation attached to their arrival in the side. Without the pillars of experience, the younger players have to make the step up from second-XI cricket to the first XI too early. Often it is not so much a step, more a leap, and it is too much for some. The development of a county side should be a seamless progression. As one experienced player departs, the colt of five years before should be ready to assume his place and another youngster brought in. Without long-term youth development, a county will stagger from one crisis to another, continually shoring up with old pros from other counties seeing out their useful working life. We were in that situation at Glamorgan not so long ago. We became a dumping ground for characters at the end of their careers. There was no development policy, no long-term planning. The work of Tom Cartwright and Alan Jones has changed all that and the Glamorgan side of 1997 was almost entirely home-grown. Sussex look as though they have players with potential. If they mature, probably alongside a good overseas professional, the circle will turn for them. Tony Pigott and the committee there at Hove know the problem and it will surely eventually work out. Having a long-term youth-development strategy will pay dividends.

I suppose that, at some stage in the future, there could be the prospect of some moneyed cricket-lover trying to buy his county success. With the freedom of contract regulations, more players will be looking to move county for greater financial reward at the end of their contracts. In football and in rugby, millionaires have set out to buy the best possible team to bring success. It could happen in cricket, but it would only bring short-term rewards. The answer, in all sports, is to build a success-ful team and, as players need to be replaced, have a youngster ready and waiting to step in. Football clubs try to emulate Manchester United, but without United's long-established youth policy, any resemblance will be purely temporary.

After two successive victories it might have been tempting to relax a little, but Duncan Fletcher insisted on discipline at all times. We still had to arrive at the ground early, and fielding routines did not alter, as he made sure that we did not become complacent or sloppy. When I was musing over whether to linger longer over the second cup of coffee, I remembered that I had said to him before the season started that if this team had discipline we could win something.

Duncan's presence in the dressing-room throughout the season was reassuring. He had the respect of everyone and is brimful of ideas but he had to come to terms with the amount of cricket we play. In South Africa, their championship is over just ten matches and for each one there is the build-up to an event. Over here, it is easy for players to become lacklustre and dull as one match follows another. That leads to a dropping-off in performance – we could not afford that.

There is one man of Glamorgan cricket that I am disappointed I never met. Emrys Davies retired nine years before I was born. Those who saw him play say that, some 30 years on and more, I resembled him with a penchant for driving straight and through the off side. Unlike him, I am no sort of bowler, with only two first-class wickets to my name. Emrys was not only the 'Rock of Glamorgan' as he opened the batting for a generation either side of the Second World War, but he also played a major part in the bowling attack with his left-arm slows. Relying more on flight than spin, he did the double twice (in 1935, the first Glamorgan player to do so) and then in 1937, when he scored over two thousand runs and took 103 wickets.

With Arnold Dyson, an exiled Yorkshireman, he formed a formidable opening partnership, with 32 century stands in ten seasons – and, remember, they were interrupted by the war in 1939, when he was 35 and Dyson 34. They could have batted together for a few more seasons. Batsmen went on a little longer in those days.

Indeed, Emrys did not retire until 1954, so he played in the front line against Larwood and Voce pre-war and Trueman and Tyson afterwards. When he finished, he had scored over 26,000 runs in more than a thousand first-class innings, hit 31 centuries and taken 885 wickets. He really was an all-time Glamorgan great.

If there is one match that typifies the man it has to be the 1937 county championship game against Leicestershire at the Aylestone Road ground they used pre-war. Davies and Dyson set a new record for Glamorgan's first wicket – 274. Dyson 126, Davies 139. But, as if to set himself apart from the ordinary mortals in the game, Emrys took a hat-trick too.

He never played for England, though he was picked for the 1939 tour of India which was called off when that German chap went on a tour of a rather more violent kind through Poland and the rest of Europe. In the 1939 season Emrys made the highest score in Glamorgan's history, 287 not out against Gloucestershire at Newport. Wally Hammond scored 302 in the same match. It must have been some batting track.

My own memories of Newport's Rodney Parade ground are not so pleasant. On the rugby side of the ground I was playing for Newport United against Gloucester, knowing that I had been lined up to play in midweek for the first team against Moseley. Then a second cartilage went and my knee problems began in earnest.

Two years later I was back, captaining Glamorgan in a Sunday League match against Gloucestershire. It looked odds-on a Glamorgan victory. At 133 for six with about four overs left needing 172, Gloucestershire's Vibert Greene came in to hammer 32 off 13 balls and we lost. Vibert was used by Gloucestershire as a stand-in when Courtney Walsh was not available. He later played league cricket in Wales; like Vasbert Drakes and Henderson Springer, they all played 'out west' in Pembrokeshire for a while.

Emrys was born and bred not quite as far west as that, in Carmarthenshire – Llanelli. He was only the second Welshman to be signed as a professional by Glamorgan. At first they did not think he would make it as a batsman or a bowler. It was Johnny Clay and Maurice Turnbull who had sufficient faith in him to make sure that he was not sacked and made the grade.

That 287 not out of Emrys Davies was at the back of my mind throughout my Glamorgan career. At first, I thought, was I good enough to make that kind of score? Then, would I ever get the opportunity to score so many? Would I have the stamina to bat that long? He batted for seven and a half hours – against Warwickshire I was in nine hours for 233 before I was interrupted by Allan Donald. QED.

After the war, Arnold Dyson was still playing, but by the championship season of 1948 he appeared in only six matches. That year, Emrys was Glamorgan's leading run-scorer, opening with Phil Clift, Gilbert Parkhouse or Dyson.

He was 50 when he retired. Halfway through the season at Peterborough he was bowled in the first over for a duck by

Frank Tyson. A few other good players at the time were beaten for pace and clean-bowled by Tyson, including Bernard Hedges, 23 years his junior, in that same over. But Emrys called time and told his captain, Wilf Wooller, 'Skipper, I'm finished – I can't see it any more.' He did not go in to bat in the second innings and never played for the county again. Instead – it always makes me smile – he became an umpire!

He stood in a couple of Tests but preferred to coach, which he did at Llandovery College and then in South Africa. He died in Llanelli in 1975 aged 71. By all accounts he was a lovely man, steeped in cricket, quiet and unassuming. I am sorry that I never met him. We would have had so much to talk about.

		M	Inns	NO	Runs	HS	Avge	100	50
D.E. DAVIES	1924–54	612	1016	79	26102	287*	27.85	31	148
A. JONES	1957–83	610	1102	71	34056	204*	33.03	52	186
H. MORRIS	1981–97	289	502	51	18520	233*	41.06	52	88

Was Larwood quicker than Donald? Where did he score his runs off the quick bowlers? He and Arnold Dyson must have been like me and Steve, just as superstitious. He scored a thousand runs 16 times for Glamorgan. Fit? He did not miss a match from 1932 to 1938.

Glamorgan 1st innings

James	c	Moores	b	Kirtley	48
Morris			lbw	Kirtley	11
Dale	c	Moores	b	Kirtley	0
Maynard	c	Moores	b	Robinson	15
Cottey			lbw	Robinson	0
Croft	c	Athey	b	Robinson	24
Shaw		not out			34
Waqar			c&b	Kirtley	7
Thomas			b	Kirtley	0
Watkin	c	Greenfield	b	Drakes	10
Cosker			lbw	Kirtley	1
Extras					22
Total: all out 53.5 overs					172

Fall: 1-30, 2-30, 3-52, 4-52, 5-98, 6-127, 7-138, 8-140, 9-171

	O	M	R	W
Drakes	16	3	56	1
Kirtley	22.5	4	60	6
Robinson	15	0	54	3

Sussex 1st innings

Pierce			lbw	Croft	6
Greenfield	c	Croft	b	Waqar	0
Taylor	c	Shaw	b	Waqar	0
Athey			lbw	Croft	7
K. Newell			b	Waqar	11
M. Newell			b	Waqar	2
Moores	c	Croft	b	Waqar	3
Drakes	c	Croft	b	Waqar	0
Khan			lbw	Waqar	0
Robinson		not out			15
Kirtley			lbw	Waqar	2
Extras					8
Total: all out 22.5 overs					54

Fall: 1-5, 2-5, 3-11, 4-16, 5-19, 6-31, 7-31, 8-35, 9-42

	O	M	R	W
Waqar	11.5	4	17	8
Watkin	3	2	4	0
Croft	8	2	25	2

Glamorgan 2nd innings

James			not out		82
Morris			b	Drakes	3
Dale	c	M. Newell	b	Drakes	6
Maynard		run out			61
Cottey	c	Moores	b	Robinson	0
Croft			lbw	Robinson	6
Shaw			lbw	Khan	0
Waqar	c	Drakes	b	Khan	5
Thomas			b	Robinson	0
Watkin			lbw	Robinson	3
Cosker		not out			0
Extras					17
Total: 9 wkts dec 48 overs					183

Fall: 1-11, 2-29, 3-148, 4-150, 5-168, 6-171, 7-177, 8-178, 9-182

	O	M	R	W
Drakes	11	2	47	2
Kirtley	9	1	37	0
Robinson	15	4	42	4
Khan	12	2	44	2
K. Newell	1	0	10	0

Sussex 2nd inning

Pierce			lbw	Croft	16
Greenfield	c	Cottey	b	Watkin	14
Taylor			lbw	Watkin	0
Athey			lbw	Thomas	7
K. Newell	c	Croft	b	Thomas	3
M. Newell			b	Croft	2
Moores			lbw	Croft	1
Drakes	c	Maynard	b	Thomas	9
Khan	c	Cottey	b	Thomas	6
Robinson			b	Thomas	0
Kirtley		not out			1
Extras					6

Total: all out 32.4 overs 67

Fall: 1-18, 2-18, 3-45, 4-49, 5-49, 6-51, 7-60, 8-60, 9-66

	O	M	R	W
Waqar	7	2	17	0
Watkin	8	2	13	2
Thomas	9.4	3	24	5
Croft	8	5	9	3

Opening for England against Sri Lanka at Lord's 1991 (© Patrick Eagar)

(*TOP*): 'What's he bowling then, Jamer?' – 'Runs!'
(© Huw John)

(*MIDDLE*): 'The next one is going to be quick.' And it was!
(© Huw Evans)

(*BOTTOM*): The helmet and the head: the helmet took half the impact of the bouncer from Donald
(© *Western Mail*)

(TOP): The Spice Boys
on tour, Caribbean
1992: Fat, Daddy, Old
and Thin Spice in
concert

(BOTTOM): 'Captain,
you'll never know
how much this means
to me.'
(© Huw John)

(LEFT): On the way out with Jamer for the last time – eleven for the title
(© Huw John)

(BELOW): Screeching with delight and sheer elation: two stumps for me, one for Watty
(© *Western Mail*)

The subdued celebration with Wicky and Darren (© Huw John)

To Wales, the championship – even Duncan is wearing a Wales rugby shirt
(© Huw John)

Glamorgan CCC 1997: (*back row, from left to right*) Evans, Tomlinson, Davies, Jones, Parkin, Powell and Law; (*middle row*) Denning, Derrick, Fletcher, Thomas, Shaw, Butcher, Jones, Lewis; (*front row*) James, Croft, Morris, Cottey, Maynard, Watkin, Metson, Dale (© Huw John)

'Are you growing that moustache for a bet?' (© *Western Mail*)

(RIGHT): The prototype Neil Jenkins: South Glamorgan Institute versus Glamorgan Wanderers, 1983 (© *Western Mail*)

(ABOVE): Mr and Mrs Morris

(LEFT): The Morris Minors, Emily and Bethan

To Lord's with a title – and a bat, just in case there's a chance of a game
(© *Western Mail*)

ELEVEN

Halfway There

Glamorgan v Gloucestershire
St Helen's, 2–5 July 1997
Britannic Assurance County Championship

		P	Pts
1.	MIDDLESEX	8	118
2.	ESSEX	7	116
3.	GLAMORGAN	8	115
4.	KENT	7	109
5.	GLOUCESTERSHIRE	8	98
6.	NOTTINGHAMSHIRE	8	91
7.	YORKSHIRE	8	85
8.	LEICESTERSHIRE	8	84
9.	HAMPSHIRE	8	83
10.	SOMERSET	8	76
11.	WORCESTERSHIRE	7	72
12.	WARWICKSHIRE	7	71
13.	SURREY	8	67
14.	DURHAM	7	65
15.	LANCASHIRE	8	58
16.	SUSSEX	8	57
17.	DERBYSHIRE	8	51
18.	NORTHAMPTONSHIRE	7	39

While the weather at Swansea had held for long enough to
enable us to beat Sussex inside three days, elsewhere there had

been torrential downpours which limited the amount of play at Headingley, where two of the title challengers, Yorkshire and Middlesex, were restricted to just four and three points respectively, and Gloucestershire only picked up three at Luton. Leicestershire and Warwickshire were wiped out completely on all four days at Grace Road, the first four-day game in this country to be abandoned without a ball being bowled.

With Essex beating Derbyshire by an innings at Southend to move up to second just behind Middlesex, it obviously proved that it was best to be beside the seaside in June. We were just hoping the rain stayed away in July.

I had scored my first-ever century against Gloucestershire at Bristol in 1996 when Steve James and I put on 240 for the first wicket, one of our best-ever stands. For the first time for Glamorgan, four of us scored centuries in one innings in that game, Steve and I, Matthew and Tony Cottey. It was a rain-affected game so that even after we had forced them to follow on, we could not press on to complete the win. Rain also caused a problem at Swansea on the first two days when just 79 overs were bowled, but in that time we had reached 319 for three and I was happily playing at somewhere near my best – 158 not out. Quite why I had suddenly rediscovered how to score runs after a set of low scores is one of those cricket imponderables. The only poor shots I had played were at Aigburth when I was double bluffed by Harvey and I was not too happy about the stroke I played when I was bowled by Vasbert Drakes at Swansea in the previous match. Through it all I felt in reasonable nick. I was not concerned about my form but by the fact the runs were not coming.

Our quick progress towards maximum batting points was largely down to Matthew's influence. Together we put on 223 for the third wicket in only 45 overs. Matthew looked odds-on for another hundred against Gloucestershire, his seventh, when he was out for 98, giving a return catch to Shaun Young, Gloucestershire's resident Aussie for the season. (Some years earlier at St Helen's, I had been out for 98 against Gloucestershire, dollying a catch back to a former Blundellian, Jeremy Lloyds.)

Why Matthew had been so successful against Gloucestershire, while I had not in the past, is another of those cricketing questions without an answer. Why was I scoring my eighth hundred at Swansea while Matthew had only ever made one championship century there?

My lust for targets and records was satisfied at St Helen's. The 173 was my 51st century for Glamorgan so just one more was required to draw level with Alan Jones's county record. I was going to be some way short of his aggregate of runs for Glamorgan for some considerable time. I did, though, move up to fourth on the all-time run-scorers list for the county when I had made 21, ahead of Arnold Dyson, but still behind Jones, Emrys Davies and Gilbert Parkhouse.

The innings against Gloucestershire was typical for me as I set landmarks and targets throughout. Double figures; then 21 to break Dyson's record; 50; then 58 to reach 700 runs for the season; 75; a hundred and then 108 to reach 750 and so on. Early in my career I made a century and then was out soon afterwards. I thought that was because I was setting the next target too high – 150 instead of 110 – and putting too much pressure on myself. It may sound selfish, but I rather like to think that it was a good method of motivation.

Without Courtney Walsh, Gloucestershire had a steady attack rather than a fearsome one. I rate Courtney as the best fast bowler in the world on a day-in, day-out basis. We have played against each other for the best part of 15 years, since the 1982 Under-19 series between the West Indies and England. We were opposing captains of the 'A' teams when England toured the Caribbean in 1992. On that tour, he hit me a nasty smack on the helmet with a bouncer. The helmet was badly dented, and was later presented to Courtney as a prize to contribute towards his benefit fund.

Against us, Mike Smith was missing because he had been called up by England for the Old Trafford Test. Though he did not subsequently play, he was released too late to join his county colleagues at Swansea, so the Gloucestershire opening bowlers were Jonathan Lewis and Shaun Young. Both medium pacers, they caused a few problems by wobbling the ball around in the heavy atmosphere early on. Steve James and Adrian Dale were both out before we reached 40 but then Matthew came in to transform the game.

Gloucestershire have a tradition of spin bowling going back to the war: Sam Cook who, sadly, died in September 1996; David Allen and John Mortimore who are still to be seen occasionally around the ground at Bristol; 'Bomber' Wells who was once told by his captain that he was making the game look 'absolutely stupid' because he bowled off one and a half paces. The latest in the line of Gloucestershire off-spinners is Martyn Ball. He is 27 now, but, like Robert Croft, has been around county cricket for almost ten years. He is a bright, intelligent cricketer who has been known to make the odd comment that betrays his two A-levels. At Hove he was quoted as saying: 'You just have to beat this lot [Sussex], don't you? Otherwise, you're a laughing stock.' The following day, in a Benson & Hedges game, Gloucestershire lost by 34 runs.

'Benny' Ball is a good county performer who has been over-shadowed by the other off-spinners around the circuit who have come through and overtaken him since he was an England Young Cricketer in 1989. Of the five regular county off-spinners who made their débuts between 1987 and 1989, it is worth noting that the man who has bowled most and, in my opinion, made most progress is Robert Croft.

	Début	Runs	Wkts	Avge	BB	50ws
M.C.J. Ball	1988	7337	195	37.63	8-46	0
J. Boiling	1988	6633	140	47.38	6-84	0
R.D.B. Croft	1989	17520	469	37.36	8-66	5
N.M.K. Smith	1987	9964	265	37.60	7-42	0
S.D. Udal	1989	12934	356	36.33	8-50	4

I hit Benny out of the attack during the game at Swansea. I felt very confident facing him as I put him away three times in succession on the leg side for boundaries. It was Duncan Fletcher who, earlier in the season, suggested that I change my method of playing off-spinners on the leg side. Instead of playing with a straight bat and driving and nudging, he thought I should use a flat bat. The three shots for four – slog, sweep and sweep – were proof that I had mastered the change. I'd say that 1997 was not a vintage season for Ball. He needs more consistency in line and greater variation in delivery to move further up the pecking order. He is a month older than Croft, but in cricketing age and experience two or three years behind, though he was picked for England at Under-19 level ahead of Croft.

Mark Alleyne, captain in the absence of Walsh and with Russell turning the job down, had done so well to keep Gloucestershire in the hunt for the title, leading by example (eventually 1,000 runs and 44 wickets). He also had the benefit of major contributions throughout the season from Mike Smith, Shaun Young and Jack Russell (999 runs and 57 dismissals). I once described Jack as being 'a few runs short of the follow-on' – he is an eccentric as everyone knows, but cricket seems to produce odd characters who are extremely able. Against us he was down to bat at seven. I am not sure that helps his England ambitions much. He was as good (if not better) with the bat than four out of the top six in the Gloucestershire batting order. A few more first-class centuries (he has only scored five for Gloucestershire) would enhance his cause even further. To do that, though, he probably needs to bat higher in the order.

Four hundred for five declared in the 103rd over was a sound enough platform. Tony Cottey had shown a welcome return to form with 76 not out; he is another of our batsmen who seems to love batting at St Helen's. He has scored five centuries there including a career best 203 and another innings of 191. It was good to see him at home again.

Cottey's 1997 was not his best season by a long way, but he remained an important cog in the Glamorgan machine. Coming in, usually at five, he is often left with the tail to work with and he has proved over the years that he is as skilful at marshalling runs from the late order as anyone in the game. He will undoubtedly score runs again and will be in many people's fantasy teams for 1998.

When Gloucestershire batted, Waqar, Watty and Cosker took three wickets each and we bowled them out well inside the follow-on target. Of the ten wickets to fall, nine went to catches. Several of the Gloucestershire batsmen had done the initial hard work and made a few runs only to be removed – usually when Matthew made a bowling change. It was a painless exercise for us, though I was beginning to wonder if I would ever have another chance come to me in the field. This was the ninth match of the season and I had caught nothing. Since the dropped chance at Headingley, nothing had even come my way.

By the close of the third day, Gloucestershire had followed on and Tony Wright had been caught off Cosker. We were looking for maximum points and the chance to go top, especially as Middlesex were struggling against Lancashire at Uxbridge having picked up only one bonus point, and Essex had been beaten by Somerset at Chelmsford by ten wickets. Curiouser and curiouser.

On the Saturday morning Gloucestershire's Nick Trainor and nightwatchman Richard Davis kept us out for over an hour – until Darren Thomas came on to replace Watty from the sea end. His third ball swung away from Trainor, took the edge and was caught by Shaw. In his next over, Davis was persuaded to touch one low to first slip and, wonder of wonders, the ball was suddenly there, safely caught in the palm of my left hand. The good work begun by Tom Cartwright during the winter in remodelling Darren's action had been continued by Duncan Fletcher. According to Darren, he was now bowling more chest-on than before – 'Like Malcolm Marshall'. The pace at times was similar. Dean Cosker whittled through the rest, though Jack Russell and Mark Alleyne held us up for 19 overs. For a while, half the Glamorgan side were thinking back to 1991 at Cheltenham when Jack batted for five hours for 79 not out to save the game for Gloucestershire with nine wickets down. This time, eventually, an edge off bat and pad carried to Matthew at short leg and Waqar came back to flatten the tail. A ten-wicket win, maximum points and, with Middlesex going down to an innings defeat at Uxbridge, we were top of the table. The two matches at St Helen's had brought us a 44-point haul, we had climbed four places and gone from 20 points behind to 13 in front.

That Saturday evening was so different to the weekend of the Middlesex match. Since then we had cantered to three resounding victories and everyone in the team had made at least one significant contribution in that time.

While at Swansea, an advertisement in *The Times* caught my

eye. The English Cricket Board was looking for a technical director as Micky Stewart was due to retire at the end of the year. I thought that just about everybody in the game who had designs to go into coaching eventually would be looking at the post and thinking it was perfect for them.

I felt I had most of the credentials required. Strange though it may seem, I had never been to a job interview and I thought that, even if I was unsuccessful, the experience of a board-type interview would be immensely useful. I had until 25 July to make up my mind about applying, but it was one of those things that, once seen, was embedded in the memory. I knew it was of great significance. I knew that I had to apply for it.

Glamorgan 1st innings

James	c	Lynch	b	Lewis	8
Morris			lbw	Lewis	173
Dale	c	Russell	b	Lewis	0
Maynard			c&b	Young	98
Cottey		not out			76
Butcher	c	Ball	b	Alleyne	0
Shaw		not out			16
Extras					29
Total: 5 wkts dec 102.3 overs					400

DNB: Waqar, Thomas, Watkin, Cosker
Fall: 1-28, 2-40, 3-263, 4-347, 5-350

	O	M	R	W
Lewis	26	3	87	3
Young	18	4	59	1
Sheeraz	7	0	40	0
Ball	19	1	76	0
Alleyne	17	1	61	1
Davis	15.3	0	70	0

Gloucestershire 1st innings

Wright	c	Butcher	b	Cosker	32
Trainor	c	James	b	Waqar	6
Hancock	c	Shaw	b	Watkin	21
Lynch	c	Maynard	b	Watkin	38
Young	c	Maynard	b	Watkin	38
Alleyne	c	Cottey	b	Cosker	0
Russell	c	Cottey	b	Cosker	22

Ball	c	Thomas	b	Watkin	12
Davis			lbw	Waqar	2
Lewis	c	Shaw	b	Thomas	20
Sheeraz		not out			12
Extras					11
Total: all out 58.4 overs					214

Fall: 1-19, 2-46, 3-93, 4-101, 5-102, 6-162, 7-170, 8-182, 9-182

	O	M	R	W
Waqar	15	2	55	3
Watkin	17	5	61	3
Cosker	18	1	59	3
Thomas	7.4	1	26	1
Cottey	1	0	2	0

Gloucestershire 2nd innings

Wright	c	Cottey	b	Cosker	28
Trainor	c	Shaw	b	Thomas	37
Davis	c	Morris	b	Thomas	15
Hancock			b	Thomas	1
Lynch			lbw	Cosker	8
Young	c	Maynard	b	Cosker	3
Alleyne			lbw	Watkin	42
Russell	c	Maynard	b	Cosker	27
Ball			b	Waqar	41
Lewis			b	Waqar	10
Sheeraz		not out			3
Extras					18
Total: all out 89.1 overs					233

Fall: 1-43, 2-84, 3-89, 4-94, 5-102, 6-103, 7-169, 8-183, 9-222

	O	M	R	W
Waqar	16.1	3	40	2
Watkin	22	8	46	1
Thomas	18	4	40	3
Cosker	27	8	87	4
Butcher	1	0	2	0
Dale	4	1	9	0
Cottey	1	1	0	0

Glamorgan 2nd innings

James	not out	26
Morris	not out	24
Extras		2
Total: 0 wkt 16.5 overs		52

	O	M	R	W
Lewis	4	1	12	0
Young	5	1	18	0
Davis	4.5	1	18	0
Ball	3	2	4	0

GLAMORGAN IN THE 1997 NAT WEST TROPHY, ROUND TWO

9.7.97   Beat Hampshire at Southampton by two wickets

Hampshire 302 for six (60 overs)

Glamorgan 304 for eight (59.4 overs)

We put Hampshire in to bat and were walloped once again by Robin Smith who crashed a typically belligerent 119. On a fine day, with a good pitch and Hampshire's bowling being reasonably kind, we expected to be able to overhaul them. Adrian Dale and I put on 128 for the second wicket, Dale 71, me 53. Then Steve James, batting down the order made 69 putting on 76 with Adrian Shaw for the seventh wicket. Shaw with his 34 not out saw it through to the end but we had to rely on Waqar hitting the winning runs in the final over as the game became far more tense than it should have been allowed to become. Nevertheless, it was a good win; everyone there enjoyed the match.

TWELVE

Daley's Day

Derbyshire v Glamorgan
Queen's Park, 23–26 July 1997
Britannic Assurance County Championship

		P	Pts
1.	GLAMORGAN	9	139
2.	ESSEX	9	126
3.	GLOUCESTERSHIRE	10	125
4.	MIDDLESEX	9	119
5.	KENT	9	117
6.	YORKSHIRE	10	117
7.	LEICESTERSHIRE	10	114
8.	LANCASHIRE	10	105
9.	WARWICKSHIRE	9	104
10.	SOMERSET	9	100
11.	NOTTINGHAMSHIRE	9	98
12.	SURREY	10	95
13.	WORCESTERSHIRE	8	94
14.	HAMPSHIRE	10	93
15.	NORTHAMPTONSHIRE	9	83
16.	DURHAM	9	72
17.	SUSSEX	10	65
18.	DERBYSHIRE	9	55

We were fortunate in 1997 to play at grounds in very pictur-
esque surroundings – Canterbury, Worcester, our own Aber-

gavenny and Chesterfield. These days Derbyshire play most of their championship games at Derby, venturing to the north of the county just once or twice a season to Chesterfield, only a couple of miles from the border with Yorkshire, but where the people are very definitely fiercely proud of their Derbyshire cricket and cricketers. The Bassetlaw League side that plays there has produced a few first-class cricketers in its time, notably Geoff Miller in recent years. Tony Borrington, Harry Cartwright, Mike Hendrick and Alan Ward also played for them.

Back in 1992 we arrived at Chesterfield to see a 'green top' prepared for Ian Bishop and Devon Malcolm. To make sure they had sufficient firepower, Derbyshire added three more seamers, Mortensen, Griffith and Warner. We had Watkin, Bastien and Dale plus a 17-year-old making his début – Darren Thomas. Of course, we lost the toss and were put in to bat. Tony Cottey batted courageously, making 62 with a fractured thumb, but even though Bishop was cautioned for bowling too many bouncers, their attack was permanently hostile and we were all out for 170. They scored almost double our total, the bonus for us being Darren Thomas's five for 80 – so he became the youngest bowler ever to take five wickets on his début. We managed to save the game with Matthew Maynard making 176 after Bishop had hit him a fearful blow on the helmet before he had got off the mark. Memories! Chesterfield was steeped in them.

While bowlers might well find some help in the pitch, if they stray off line and length, it can become a very quick-scoring ground. This time we won the toss, put Derbyshire in and at the close of the first day they were 379 for four. Waqar, Watkin and Thomas were all nursing injured bowling figures. With Croft away with England at Headingley, the spin bowling was in the hands of Dean Cosker and he at least put the brakes on. Deep into the second day, worn out and with weary, flat feet, about the only thing to be thankful for was Cosker's one for 79 from 38 overs, as Derbyshire had rattled along to 513 for six declared. Both their openers scored centuries, Adrian Rollins crashing it everywhere in his 148 and Michael May, Chesterfield-born, following suit with 116 as they put on 247 for the first wicket. This was not only a first-wicket record for Derbyshire against us, but a record for any wicket – and it felt like it.

We were thoroughly outplayed by Derbyshire. In 1996 at Cardiff they had murdered us in early May and given a clear indication that they were championship material. John Owen and Colin Wells had both scored centuries, we declared behind and were set 218 to win in 62 overs but it was one of those days when it all went right for Devon Malcolm. Before we knew where we were, the score was 48 for five and eventually we lost by 110 runs. The surprise at Chesterfield was that they had suddenly come good when they were in such turmoil. Captain, coach and chairman had all resigned, Dean Jones's departure had left them without an overseas professional and Dominic Cork was not fit for championship cricket. There were frequent ructions over Kim Barnett giving interviews to the media outlining the players' attitude to the goings-on, and Chris Adams still wanted to leave the club. Derbyshire are not new to such problems but rarely have they occurred with such ferocity and volume.

We looked likely to follow on against them until Adrian 'Arthur' Dale just refused to be dislodged. He had scored 106 in the first match of the season against Warwickshire, but had drifted in and out of form since then, just six runs in his three innings prior to Chesterfield.

The youngsters, Mike Powell and Alun Evans, were no doubt starting to anticipate a call-up but Dale's 142 not out saved the follow on and earned us the maximum batting points, increased the next day when the rain came in from the Peak District to condemn the game to a draw. In a way, this was a tribute to our resilience as a side; previous Glamorgan teams would have folded twice and lost heavily.

Andrew Harris, the 24-year-old Derbyshire pace bowler, made such a good impression in 1996 when he took 53 first-class wickets, but he had been struggling for form throughout the season. The off-field shenanigans had perhaps not helped him much. He took two wickets against us but, like Chris Silverwood at Yorkshire earlier in the season, he appeared to have lost a touch of sharpness from his approach generally and he was not the bowler who took my wicket twice the year before at Cardiff.

Perhaps he just needed a wise old head to offer a little guidance. There ought to be a few knowledgeable fast bowlers around Derbyshire to help out – they have certainly bred enough over the years. When I first started in county cricket, the line of Derbyshire-born fast bowlers had temporarily halted, so they imported the best available at the time – Michael Holding. But, seemingly from nowhere, another generation of seamers arrived: Cork, then Harris and Aldred. Talk to anyone around the county grounds of Derbyshire and the first topic of conversation is certain to be opening bowlers. I made only one century in Derbyshire and thought I had done well against Cork and Malcolm, only to be told on an excursion around the boundary that I 'wouldn't have lasted five minutes against Brian Jackson'.

'A second-XI player on his way up,' I thought. Later in the evening I mentioned the name to a journalist from Derby. 'Brian Jackson,' he said, 'is a legend round here – played in the 1960s and took wickets by the hatful for nowt at all.'

I checked. He took 457 wickets in six seasons at an average of 18. Furthermore, *Wisden* one season said that he 'fell away disappointingly'. He had taken 63 wickets at an average of 16! He was a genuine number 11 but, having criticised the batsmen for giving him nothing to bowl at, his captain put him up the order to number four. Caught off David Steele for nine. Look it up if you do not believe me. Northants v Derbyshire 1965.

Meanwhile, the book of the week at Chesterfield was Mike Carey's biography of Les Jackson, the 'greatest bowler Derbyshire has ever known' – which is some accolade. Les, apparently, was different class, taking over 100 wickets ten times in the seasons between 1949 and 1962 but playing only twice for England – in 1949 and 1961. Colin Cowdrey thought that Jackson was a great bowler who should have played more often for England. 'By unshakeable tradition, fast bowlers picked for Test matches are genuinely fast. Thus over a period of five years Trueman and Statham were automatically selected for matches at Lord's when they were not necessarily the best bowlers suited to the conditions. Lord's during those years was a seamer's paradise and had England picked Les Jackson, plus Derek Shackleton and Tom Cartwright, we would have been more successful. Against those three men I would not have backed a visiting team, whatever its reputation, to make above 200 in an innings more than once in 20 attempts. The trouble was, we never had the courage to come to terms with seam bowling.'

It is only recently that we have come to terms with picking Test sides to match the conditions. I'm thinking particularly of games at Headingley where Steve Watkin and Neil Mallender have been called up as the most effective bowlers for certain conditions. Talk to Don Shepherd about life on the county circuit in the 1960s and it seems that there were more good bowlers around than today. It is no wonder, really, that Jackson could not make a place in the England team his own when he was competing against the likes of Trueman, Statham, Tyson and Bedser. Shep himself, despite his 2,000 wickets for Glamorgan, did not win a single cap because he was up against Laker, Lock, Wardle, Illingworth, Titmus and Allen. Having seen Shep in the nets – even well after his 60th birthday – it is obvious that he was a very good bowler. From reading about his generation it seems that an England attack of Jackson, Shackleton, Shepherd and Cartwright would have given nothing away and, provided the Mays, Cowdreys and Dexters did not play any daft shots, England would have won every Test match! Fred Trueman says Jackson should have played 'in 20 or 30 Tests' and that he understood the reason for his continued exclusion as Gubby Allen's refusal to pick him because he did not have a classic, side-on action.

Having heard through the grapevine that Lord's did not approve of Jackson's 'ugly' action, Derbyshire sent him to Alf Gover, the coach in Surrey, to see if any aesthetic improvement could be made. Gover said that he could help him gain an extra yard of pace but did not want to meddle with the basic action because it was so effective in generating considerable movement off the pitch.

It is always fascinating for me to read of cricket played in eras past. The days of Les Jackson and Don Shepherd are from the black-and-white generation; we need Mike Carey and his colleagues to put them into colour and perspective.

Shep as a coach was not one for meddling if an action proved effective. Advice, as he has been offering over the years to Robert Croft and Steve Watkin, is more valuable than tinkering with an approach unless something has gone seriously wrong. Shep's spin partner in the famous 1964 victory over the Australians at Swansea was Jim Pressdee – a fine all-rounder from Swansea who later emigrated to South Africa. Between them the two spinners took 19 wickets in the match. Yet in 1962 Pressdee had lost form to such an extent that he claimed only one wicket in the championship. In 1963 and 1964 he took a hundred wickets in each season as he completed successive doubles. What had made the difference? Pressdee himself told Fred Trueman that when he had joined the staff as a teenager, coaches had taken one look at his action and changed it. He did not use his original action again until he went to South Africa in 1962. Bowling a few balls with his natural action, he found that he was immediately successful. According to Fred, 'Coaching is disastrous if it kills a man's natural style. Once you do that, you ruin what potential was there.' Fred is, of course, right. A complete natural himself, nobody 'taught' him to bowl fast, but there must have been times when, for whatever reason, he could not produce his best. A good coach will be able to spot the problem, whether it be physical, mental or technical, and put it right; but once a player knows how to bowl and can do so effectively, a complete overhaul is not necessary. David Leadbetter rebuilt Nick Faldo's golf swing to good effect, but in cricket it appears that such a drastic move only disrupts natural talent. By contrast, Darren Thomas was going nowhere with his original action and only really emerged after a 'revamp'.

Nottinghamshire were without a game and on the Friday their captain drove over the short distance from his home near Newark to sit on our balcony for a couple of hours and watch us struggling against the Derbyshire attack. Paul Johnson was wrestling with a problem. He was due to meet Andy Pick later that afternoon to discuss his future with the county. Pick, Johnson and Morris all came into county cricket at around the same time. We had played for Young England against Young Australia at Chelmsford in 1983. I remember thinking then that someone had done a good job at Trent Bridge to marshal all the young talent as another Notts colt, Peter Such, took seven Australian wickets. Johno was a pocket battleship of a batsman – still is, actually – with a lot to say for himself, but he was mortified when he somehow managed to squirt cold spray into Picky's eye in the dressing-room. He thought he might have blinded him, or at least put him out of the game. In the end all was well.

Despite that, the two have been close friends for years. We all went on the England 'A' tour to Bermuda and the West Indies in 1991–92. So many friendships have been forged between professional players on tours abroad.

Because of injury, Picky played only six matches in 1996 and just two in 1997. Johno had the unenviable task of telling his old mate that his contract was not going to be renewed. He could have left the job to his cricket manager, but, typical of Johno, he opted to break the news in person. It is never an easy thing to do: almost certainly there would have been a few tears shed, but it does avoid the embarrassment that Glamorgan suffered when, at the end of 1996, Steve Barwick, Neil Kendrick and Alistair Dalton were told that they were about to be released in the middle of a second-XI match at Barnt Green. The trio consequently refused to field the next day and the club learned some lessons in the art of diplomacy.

Glamorgan are not the only county to have erred in this respect. Derbyshire in 1992 sacked Andrew Brown and Steve Goldsmith but the first the two players heard about it was on the local radio. Communication remains a problem in county cricket.

At the team meal on the Friday evening at Chesterfield, Don Shepherd was in great form, at his argumentative best, discussing the relative merits of bowlers past and present, with some especial emphasis on off-spinners – Saqlain Mushtaq, Surrey's overseas signing in particular.

I could sense that it was going to be one of those nights when Shep would not give an inch and was prepared to argue that night was day. I was sitting next to Waqar and, mischievously, introduced him into the conversation. Waqar proceeded to explain how Saqlain bowled his famous 'mystery' ball which spins the opposite way though it is still bowled with an off-spinner's grip. 'Rubbish!' cried Shep, who then spent the next three hours explaining why this delivery was physically impossible. I had long since left the conversation to enjoy a very acceptable bottle of Beaujolais with my room-mate Steve Watkin.

Chesterfield did not turn out to be the setting for one of the outstanding performances of the season. Few of us remember Chesterfield '97 fondly, especially Matthew Maynard who contracted chicken pox and was rated extremely doubtful for our Nat West quarter-final with Yorkshire.

Derbyshire 1st innings

Rollins	c	James	b	Cosker	148
May	c	James	b	Watkin	116
Adams			b	Waqar	46
Barnett	c	Shaw	b	Waqar	29
Vandrau	c	Maynard	b	Watkin	30
Harris	c	Shaw	b	Watkin	11
Clarke		not out			76
Krikken		not out			30
Extras					27
Total: 6 wkts dec 133 overs					513

DNB: DeFreitas, Aldred, Malcolm

Fall: 1-247, 2-324, 3-345, 4-372, 5-391, 6-429

	O	M	R	W
Waqar	28	3	132	2
Watkin	33	5	131	3
Butcher	9	3	36	0
Thomas	15	2	84	0
Dale	8	2	33	0
Cosker	38	14	79	1
Maynard	2	0	8	0

Glamorgan 1st innings

James			lbw	DeFreitas	25
Morris			lbw	DeFreitas	11
Thomas	c	Vandrau	b	Harris	31
Dale		not out			142
Maynard	c	Rollins	b	Vandrau	43
Cottey		run out			14
Butcher	c	Clarke	b	DeFreitas	22

Shaw			b	Malcolm	38
Waqar	c	Barnett	b	Harris	8
Watkin		not out			10
Extras					20
Total: 8 wkts dec 100.5 overs					364

DNB: Cosker

Fall: 1-31, 2-54, 3-88, 4-151, 5-175, 6-222, 7-312, 8-343

	O	M	R	W
Malcolm	23	2	84	1
DeFreitas	24	3	86	3
Vandrau	21	5	68	1
Harris	17.5	4	61	2
Aldred	10	3	30	0
Clarke	5	0	25	0

Derbyshire 2nd innings

Rollins	not out		24
May	not out		8
Extras			3
Total: 0 wkt 14.1 overs			35

	O	M	R	W
Waqar	5	0	17	0
Watkin	6	2	11	0
Cosker	3.1	1	4	0

GLAMORGAN IN THE 1997 NAT WEST TROPHY, QUARTER-FINAL

29.7.97   Beat Yorkshire at Cardiff by one wicket

          Yorkshire 236 for eight (60 overs)

          Glamorgan 237 for nine (59 overs)

A great bowling performance, especially from Dean Cosker (three for 26), restricted Yorkshire to a total of eminently reasonable proportions as far as we were concerned. Darren Lehmann played magnificently for his 105 and rescued them from 72 for four.

I went early, followed by Dale. Maynard and Croft pulled us round. Matthew was really too ill to play – his team talk was given with him on the balcony outside the dressing-room and the rest of us inside. Croft made 55 opening the batting,

Matthew 62 (shrugging off chicken pox, according to one paper) but we were out of it at 209 for nine. Waqar had been dropped too when he had just come in. It might have been all over, but Waqar drove at anything up to him, Cosker defended so well and somehow we beat them with an over to spare.

It was a tense, thrilling game of cricket watched by a capacity crowd at Sophia Gardens, who must have thought, as we all did, that the 28 added for the last wicket was one of the most valuable contributions to Glamorgan's season – it showed the spirit in the side (in Waqar and Cosker, actually) to keep going even though the odds were stacked in favour of the opposition.

Through to the semi-finals, Lord's beckoned.

THIRTEEN

Laughs with
the Little Fireman

Glamorgan v Nottinghanshire
Colwyn Bay, 31 July, 1–4 August 1997
Britannic Assurance County Championship

		P	Pts
1.	GLOUCESTERSHIRE	11	149
2.	GLAMORGAN	10	148
3.	KENT	10	138
4.	ESSEX	10	134
5.	MIDDLESEX	10	123
6.	LEICESTERSHIRE	11	123
7.	YORKSHIRE	10	117
8.	LANCASHIRE	11	113
9.	WARWICKSHIRE	10	112
10.	SOMERSET	10	110
11.	NOTTINGHAMSHIRE	10	108
12.	SURREY	11	105
13.	HAMPSHIRE	11	103
14.	WORCESTERSHIRE	9	102
15.	NORTHAMPTONSHIRE	10	92
16.	DURHAM	10	74
17.	SUSSEX	10	65
18.	DERBYSHIRE	10	65

Glamorgan has always been a wandering county – extending the boundaries of cricketing influence far and wide, but suggesting that a ground 200 miles from base is within 'home' territory is surely stretching it a little too far.

Back in 1966 the club at Colwyn Bay offered Glamorgan a break-even retainer of £400 to play a home match. Derbyshire were the chosen attraction – Brian Jackson and all – but they were beaten by 63 runs and Glamorgan have played there on a semi-regular basis ever since.

In 1993 and 1994, when Durham and Lancashire were the visitors, the opposition fans discovered that it was cheaper to join Glamorgan as a member than pay at the gate for all four days of championship cricket and the Sunday League. Consequently, Glamorgan's membership figure was increased and some of the new recruits became supporters in exile. Good business all round.

For the Glamorgan players, travelling to Colwyn Bay is frequently more difficult than it is for the away team. Lancashire were certainly nearer than we were. Notts probably were too. We have tried various ways of easing the travel time – flying, for instance; we have also used a team coach; some players opt for the scenic route north, through central Wales and on via Snowdonia; while the rest of us swear by the motorways – M4, M5, M6, M55 – and hope to avoid the caravans.

No other county has such a trek to a home game but, once there, it is one of the most enjoyable fixtures on the calendar. The club had chosen to make the match against Notts an 'away day' for the whole staff. The team and all the office personnel were booked into the same hotel in Llandudno. It was a strange feeling to be so far away from home, yet with so much support and so many familiar faces around.

There was one familiar face returning to the scene after eight years away – Phil North. The captain of the Wales Minor Counties side, Phil was called into our squad as Dean Cosker was required by the England Under-19s for the internationals with Zimbabwe.

In the press Matthew lambasted England for calling up fully fledged county cricketers to play in what he called 'kiddies cricket'. Cosker was not the only one; David Sales of Northants and Ben Hollioake were also involved. What we have to remember, though, is that the England Under-19 side is the pinnacle of the development of excellence and it is important that our best players in that age group be brought together to play against their peers from other countries. We must, however, always be aware of the stage of development of each individual. Perhaps certain players would benefit more from playing in a first-class county game. It is a tricky question and requires sympathetic handling.

The Glamorgan management team had been debating the type of wicket that should be made to order at Colwyn Bay. We decided that a pitch which was likely to give a degree of turn would give us the best chance of completing a victory in another 'must win' match. We were without Cosker, but Croft was back amongst us and we would always back him against the Notts off-spinner Richard Bates who was of the 'flat' variety and did not turn it much. Notts' two left-armers who were capable of spinning it considerably, Jimmy Hindson and Andy Afford, appeared to be out of favour. Croft and Cosker would have been a formidable pair to combat on a 'bunsen'. As it was, we had to bring back North, who had made his début alongside Matthew in 1985. In 22 matches he took 24 wickets at an average of 42 and last played in 1989, but in the absence of Cosker, North's slow left-armers seemed the next best option. We had no idea he would let us down.

Phil was rooming with me and I stuck to my usual routine the night before a match starts – in bed by ten. I could not sleep because there was no sign of Phil and I kept expecting him to come through the door at any moment. It was late when he did arrive and by then I was seething, which, of course, meant I had no chance of a decent night's sleep.

At the ground in the morning, we began our warm-up exercises but there was no sighting of Phil. When he eventually did show up, pleading a late alarm call, we had already declared a side and his chance of a return to big-time cricket had gone. It would have been a record for Glamorgan – eight seasons between first-class appearances. Now he had a record he did not want. Notts, meanwhile, had turned up without Bates but with two left-arm spinners in Jimmy Hindson and Usman Afzaal. Paul Johnson won the toss and batted. If it did turn, they had the advantage.

In the days of Rice and Hadlee, Notts were one of the most powerful teams in the land. Later, they were still strong but did not seem to believe in themselves and all too often were negative, preferring to avoid defeat rather than going for the win. Johno had served his apprenticeship under Clive Rice and at times his flamboyant attitude to the game seemed at odds with Notts' otherwise dour approach. In late 1993 when he was uncertain about signing on again at Trent Bridge, we at Glamorgan declared an interest. In the end he did not move, but the prospect of Maynard and Johnson in harness for Glamorgan would have given the opposition bowlers nightmares.

On the West Indies tour with England 'A', Johno was the star of the show. The management thought he was the man most likely to, but it never worked out. We talk a lot about the game when we meet. It was sad to see him turn up at Colwyn Bay with a few selection problems and players who had yet to prove themselves to him that they were worth a place in the side.

The first day was lost to rain. The second was rain-affected but, without any of the bowlers over-extending themselves, we had them nine down.

That evening over a beer I mentioned to Johno that Saturday at Colwyn Bay was always a day for entertainment. It was almost a month since I had made a decent score and my mind was set on runs aplenty in front of a good crowd.

The following morning I swiped a very long hop to deep fine leg and was caught for 12. The 'Little Fireman' at cover point was reduced to hysterical laughter as I trudged off to the pavilion. Even though I did not turn to face him I knew that it was Johno who shouted after me, 'Great entertainment, Banners!'

He was christened the Little Fireman by the former Sussex captain, Paul Parker. It was for no other reason than that he looked like Fireman Wally in the old television series *Casey Jones*. Johno says, without fear of contradiction, that he is all of five feet seven inches tall, but then Glamorgan's short but sturdy Tony Cottey owns up to being five feet five (and they are supposed to be the same height), so one of them is a liar. Appearances deceive: Johno may waddle to the wicket and play some outrageous shots, but he has a brain that is finely tuned for cricket. Clive Rice reckoned that he was thinking like a captain before he was 20. Now he has a chance to put his theories into practice.

At this stage of the season we were a point adrift of Gloucestershire but we were actually more concerned about Kent, ten points behind but with a game in hand. Going into the last third of the season we needed to stay in touch and once again Notts was one of our 'must win' games. The loss of the first day did not help.

It was Steve James, of course, who ensured that we picked up maximum batting points and in quick time too. His 162 continued a run of remarkable scores against Notts – he obviously likes their bowling. I would have done so too if I had not got myself out in ridiculous fashion to a rank bad ball. Jamer, meantime, made his third century in four innings against Notts. With Gary Butcher and Adrian Shaw laying about them effectively late on, we declared after 83 overs.

Notts' New Zealand all-rounder, Nathan Astle, brought in at the last minute when their Pakistan pace bowler Mohammad Zahid was found to have a serious back injury, was their most effective bowler with his little seamers. Not as quick as Chris Cairns, his predecessor at Notts, but in a wet summer made for swingers and cutters he was doing a good job.

On Saturday evening I enjoyed the company of Johno again for a few beers and, strolling back to the hotel, mused that I would miss the chat and banter between professionals, the gossip and the camaraderie that develops after a few years in the game and a couple of tours. I had decided to apply for the job of Technical Director at Lord's. It was a sobering thought that it might be my last season of county cricket.

Llandudno, where we stayed for the game, and Colwyn Bay, where we played, are two towns of totally different character. Llandudno, with its sea front and pier, has the bright lights and entertainment. Colwyn Bay is more sedate and residential. I do not know why, but holiday-makers from Liverpool seem to stay in Llandudno, while those from Manchester are usually to be found in Colwyn Bay. For the cricket week, though, there was a huge number of Glamorgan supporters from North and Mid Wales, giving credence to the belief that we are a national team as well as a county side.

Robert Croft had returned from the Test matches in sanguine mood. England were employing him in a defensive role, not many wickets were coming his way and chances that were offered had been dropped. The Australian pace bowlers were probing his weakness against the short ball and suddenly it had turned rather sour for him. He was not about to give in, though. He began to work hard in the nets to improve his technique and quizzed the rest of us about how to cope with the quicks. The words of Alan Jones sprang to mind immediately: 'None of us likes it, Crofty, just try not to show it.'

He cheered up immensely when he was installed in the Gorsedd of Bards at the National Eisteddfod at Bala. Proud as he was at joining the likes of Alan Jones, Ieuan Evans and Ray Gravell in the Bardic Circle, he was overjoyed to find that the only way of getting him to and from Bala in time to play was by helicopter. What a way to go over Snowdon.

On Sunday morning there was a rush to find a radio that worked. Somebody had started the rumour that Steve James was about to be named in the England side for Trent Bridge. Eventually, in a car outside the hotel, we heard that England had indeed made changes. Mark Butcher had been dropped but there was no call-up for Steve James or for Glamorgan's other opener who happened to be a left-hander. Alec Stewart would be keeping wicket and opening again, the Hollioakes were in, Croft was retained, Mike Smith had gone after one Test and Caddick was back. I was not surprised that I was not in the squad. Graham Gooch had said in a magazine article that if it was a choice between recalling me or 'giving youth its fling, then youth will win because that player will be around for another ten years'. Gooch was 41 when he played his last Test but maybe he was a rare breed. In any case, I was out of form. Apart from that 173 against Gloucestershire, I had not passed 50 in eight innings. It was back to the videos and the nets to try to capture that early-season promise again.

The Sunday at Colwyn Bay was a day of rest for one or two of us more senior players. Matthew decided to give 'youth its fling' and Watty and I were on 12th-man duties for the Sunday League game as Powell, Evans and Parkin came in. Of course, we did everything a 12th man should do, showing the youngsters the benefit of our experience from the England tours!

On the Monday, Notts were 110 for six, still 41 behind, but we failed to take wickets quickly enough after that. Tolley and Hindson, with a determined eighth-wicket partnership, batted them out of range. It was a subdued trip back down south. We should have won the game. Privately I was wondering if we were in danger of falling between twin objectives – the Lord's final and the championship.

At the end of the game Johno had come over to me as I left the field and said, 'Sorry about that, Banners – hope you go on to win it, good luck!' We were the popular choice for the championship and, as much as we had needed the win to keep up our challenge, I knew that Notts had needed a battling performance to keep pride intact in a difficult season.

Nottinghamshire 1st innings

Dowman	c	Dale	b	Waqar	62
Robinson			b	Waqar	8
Astle	c	Shaw	b	Watkin	47
Johnson			lbw	Watkin	1
Archer			c&b	Croft	10
Afzaal	c	Cottey	b	Croft	3
Tolley			b	Thomas	10
Noon		not out			29
Evans			lbw	Croft	1
Hindson			b	Waqar	0
Bowen	c	Shaw	b	Thomas	19
Extras					12
Total: all out 65.1 overs					202

Fall: 1-21, 2-71, 3-79, 4-108, 5-112, 6-131, 7-158, 8-160, 9-163

	O	M	R	W
Waqar	18	3	66	3
Watkin	12	3	46	2
Croft	24	8	46	3
Thomas	11.1	2	37	2

Glamorgan 1st innings

James	c	Hindson	b	Evans	162
Morris	c	Evans	b	Hindson	12
Dale			lbw	Astle	20
Maynard	c	Robinson	b	Afzaal	13
Cottey			lbw	Astle	0
Croft			b	Evans	31
Butcher		not out			48
Shaw		not out			31
Extras					36
Total: 6 wkts dec 83 overs					353

DNB: Waqar, Watkin, Thomas

Fall: 1-57, 2-112, 3-139, 4-140, 5-236, 6-287

	O	M	R	W
Evans	17	1	52	2
Bowen	10	1	48	0
Tolley	13	3	44	0
Hindson	20	0	101	1
Astle	10	1	39	2
Afzaal	13	4	43	1

Nottinghamshire 2nd innings

Dowman			lbw	Waqar	6
Robinson			b	Croft	4
Astle	c	Morris	b	Watkin	13
Johnson	c	Maynard	b	Croft	6
Archer	c	Dale	b	Croft	40
Afzaal			b	Thomas	10
Tolley		not out			73
Noon			lbw	Butcher	17
Evans			b	Butcher	0
Hindson		not out			42
Extras					28
Total: 8 wkts 92 overs					239

Fall: 1-8, 2-14, 3-26, 4-32, 5-74, 6-110, 7-159, 8-159

	O	M	R	W
Waqar	19	3	62	1
Croft	30	5	52	3
Watkin	13	8	27	1
Thomas	15	2	55	1
Butcher	9	2	18	2
Maynard	1	0	1	0

GLAMORGAN IN THE NAT WEST TROPHY 1997, SEMI-FINAL

12/13.8.97   Lost to Essex at Chelmsford by one wicket.

Glamorgan 301 for eight (60 overs)

Essex 303 for nine (55 overs)

It was my fourth semi-final and I lost the lot. After this season's two cliff-hangers that we had won, this went the other way but will be remembered for the unsavoury bad-tempered incidents that occurred during the game. Once again I was out early, caught in the gully, but Jamer was in great form for his 109 and, with Tony Cottey making 56, we thought that 301 for eight was a reasonable total – not out of reach, but defendable.

Stuart Law, though, played as if it were a mere handful of runs to knock off. He just produced shot after brilliant shot – 90 off 73 balls as he and Darren Robinson cantered to 150 for the first wicket in 24 overs. Law and Thomas became agitated when Thomas bowled a beamer, accidentally, and when Darren's arm went up in celebration of Irani being given out LBW, he clipped Irani on the helmet which provoked another angry exchange. Play continued till ten past eight when the light became too bad to go on. Essex wanted six to win with two wickets remaining and 6.5 overs were left. Robert Croft and Mark Ilott then had a disagreement over the state of play and the light. There were some words exchanged and a push and a little jostling, all watched in amazement by the rest of us and the wives of the two protagonists who were sitting together in front of the pavilion. The most astonishing aspect of the whole affair is that Ilott and Croft have always been great pals. The timing of the incident, after Nasser Hussain had called for more aggression in the 'cosy' world of county cricket, was more than unfortunate.

The match was decided the following morning when Peter Such, of all people, drove through the covers for the winning runs.

Four semis, four defeats – a blot on the copybook.

FOURTEEN

Second Down and Five

Worcestershire v Glamorgan
New Road, 15–18 August 1997
Britannic Assurance County Championship

		P	Pts
1.	KENT	12	171
2.	GLAMORGAN	11	159
3.	GLOUCESTERSHIRE	12	158
4.	ESSEX	12	147
5.	MIDDLESEX	11	145
6.	YORKSHIRE	11	137
7.	LANCASHIRE	12	137
8.	WARWICKSHIRE	12	137
9.	WORCESTERSHIRE	10	135
10.	LEICESTERSHIRE	13	132
11.	SURREY	12	129
12.	SOMERSET	11	118
13.	NOTTINGHAMSHIRE	11	114
14.	HAMPSHIRE	12	108
15.	NORTHAMPTONSHIRE	12	104
16.	DURHAM	12	98
17.	SUSSEX	12	89
18.	DERBYSHIRE	11	71

Terry Venables, who should know something about coaching at
the top level, outlined his philosophy once: 'You won't make bad

players into good players, but you can help excellence if you think enough about it.' So much of any game is played in the head, individually and collectively. Anyone who has played in a team will be aware of the sensation that surges through a side when suddenly each player feels impregnable. It usually starts because one person has achieved a state of real confidence and that becomes infectious. The secret for players and coaches is to retain that feeling throughout a season or over a campaign. It is as hard to retain as it is easy to lose. It is an ethereal feeling that can vanish in cricket as soon as one batsman is bowled by a big in-swinger or a slip catch dropped at a crucial time.

Quite why my form disappeared midway through the season remains a mystery to me. One day I came off the field against Gloucestershire having scored 197 runs for once out in the match, we had won by ten wickets and were top of the table having beaten one of the title contenders. Just over a month later I was preparing to play against Worcestershire on one of my favourite grounds and I was picking up the bat with a feeling of total insecurity. Form can be fickle over a long season and I have been through bad runs before, so I tried to use familiar methods to build up that elusive confidence once more.

I reminded myself continually of my earlier good form and performances, constantly ran and re-ran through my mind instances where I had played well, hit boundaries off Donald and kept out good deliveries from McCague, and then I would study videos of more recent innings, concentrating on observing the backlift. In my experience, I find that I have invariably lost form because the timing of my pick-up has gone awry.

Worcestershire were one of the counties that I might have joined when I was considering my future at the end of the 1995 season. Most county cricketers will declare that New Road is one of their favourite grounds, and it has long been a candidate for the top of 'My Best Ground Ever Played On' list. The setting is just perfect and the view from the dressing-rooms across to the cathedral so timeless, but for me, as far as scoring runs is concerned, New Road has not been especially kind.

I scored one of the early centuries of my career there in 1986, but apart from 1992 have made few runs since. That was a situation that had to be rectified if I was to prevent my average going into freefall. I had to think about where and how I was going to make runs, whereas earlier in the season, I had the in-built sense of knowing that I had a shot for any ball that was bowled at me.

We were condemned to a day in the field when we lost the toss and Tim Curtis, in controlled fashion, compiled 160. Unusually, he outscored Graeme Hick in their partnership of 178 for the second wicket. Perhaps he was 'demob-happy' after he had announced that it was to be his last season of first-class cricket.

With 342 for four at the end of the first day, it could have been worse, but Robert Croft (39-11-80-3) always seemed to have things under control. Even so, there was a danger that we might have been batted out of the match by lunch on the second day.

As it was, we ended up facing 472 for nine declared. Waqar with one for 86 and Watty none for 80 returned unfamilar figures. Once again our championship ambitions were about to be tested. If ever there was an apt time for the return of H. Morris, vintage 1990, this was it.

But it was not to be. Steve James opened in fluent fashion. I could barely hit it off the square. There is always a temptation when things are not going well to get out and give someone else a chance. I have always believed that it is better to graft for runs and stay there until the timing and general confidence returns. I tried to give Steve as much of the strike as possible and, in two extremely contrasting styles, we put on 43 for the first wicket. Then Sheriyar, left arm over, medium fast from the Diglis End, bowled a fairly innocuous length ball, outside the off stump. If I had been in good form I would quite simply have left it alone, but as I was at odds with my game, I tried to 'feel' the ball on the bat. I nicked it to slip and was caught for four.

At this point, in the afternoon of the second day, I felt at rock bottom. We had not won for two games and had been outbatted in one of them. In my last three innings, I had contributed a measly 27.

The opening partnership for any team is vital and suddenly I felt as though I was letting down Jamer, myself and the team.

When Steve and I performed well, the team generally had enough runs. As I changed out of my batting gear in the dressing-room and looked out, somewhat blankly at that lovely aspect across the ground to the cathedral, I saw Adrian Dale and Mike Powell dismissed in quick succession and that we were soon struggling at 78 for three. We had been fielding for 146 overs and only Steve James was able to concentrate fully and play in his usual manner. Then he went, caught at the wicket for 69. Butcher and Shaw were out too and at 155 for six, the follow-on target was drifting hopelessly out of reach.

Matthew was at the wicket. All season he had looked as though he was about to reduce an attack to sawdust but apart from his hundred against Durham he had not flourished in the extravagant way we all know he can. In Croft he found a partner of durability and he stepped up a gear to hit Worcestershire all over New Road. If there is a finer sight in cricket than Matthew Maynard in full flow then I want to see it.

With scant regard for length or line, he produced stroke after brilliant stroke with a succession of those trademark drives through the offside and straight. He raced to his century off 81 balls. The rest of us on the balcony and in the dressing-room were totally transfixed. It was a glittering display. Croft, Thomas and then Waqar stayed with him and by the close we were 355 for eight with Matthew 140 not out. In two hours the whole complexion of the game had been changed and the mood in the dressing-room was transformed. Worcestershire came off the field looking like we had the day before, and Tom Graveney, one of the most generous and genial men in county cricket, congratulated Matthew on an innings which, he said, ranked alongside the best he had ever seen at New Road. Praise indeed, considering that Tom has seen the best of D'Oliveira, Botham, Hick and Moody plus various opposition batsmen of some repute like May and Cowdrey. In the bar that evening, one Worcestershire supporter of a certain age said it was the best that he had seen there other than by a Worcestershire player since Gary Sobers scored 90 odd not out for Notts in a one-day game when hardly anyone else made double figures.

I have seen Matthew destroy attacks on numerous occasions:

1991 against Hampshire at Southampton was rather spectacular.

For most of the season, Worcestershire were without Newport and Illingworth. Their opening bowlers against us, Sheriyar and Mirza, suffered from the Maynard assault, but so did the 'pillar of experience' in their seam attack, Lampitt.

As usual there was plenty of support for Glamorgan around the ground. The Balconiers had made their trip up for the match and, with the ground being within easy reach of Mid Wales, there were many of our members and supporters there from Montgomeryshire and Radnorshire; it is a pity that we only play at New Road once every two years. It is one of those fixtures that we would be content to play every season. I know that Yorkshire supporters feel the same about their matches at Worcester and at Lord's and Canterbury too. In the future, if the change to divisions or conferences does take place, such fixtures would be even less frequent.

We reached 398 off only 68.4 overs – Matthew was brilliant and Waqar partnered him to add 100 for the ninth wicket. In scoring the runs so quickly we were back in the game. Watty and Waqar kept Worcestershire bottled up in their second innings and we were left 81 overs to score 374 to win. It was more than we wanted to chase, ideally, but if Steve and I could make a decent start then Matthew could make nonsense of any target. We opened with 115. I was still not happy with the way I was playing, but at least I felt I was starting to time the ball better when I was run out for 37. Curses! The communication between Steve and me failed for once. He hit into the covers and called and I suppose he was right, there was one – two halves! I was not even in the frame.

Another mini-collapse, with Dale out for 13 and Powell for a duck – a pair on his championship début, what a difference from 200 at The Parks. Worse still, Matthew was caught behind off Haynes for nought. Catastrophe!

With Steve James around we had a chance. He was in control, keeping the scoreboard moving and pushing the ball into the gaps adroitly. Then Croft and Butcher were out and the game started to drift away from us. Steve made a great 130 and Waqar batted well again but, on reflection, we kept going for the win much longer than we should have done and we were all out well short. It was a lesson we bore in mind later in the season.

Three matches without a win. Another victory was required urgently, especially as Kent, Yorkshire, Surrey and now Worcestershire were starting to pick up the pace. Gloucestershire were still up there too, having beaten Sussex. We had five games left to play.

Worcestershire, although their bowling was depleted by the injuries to Newport and Illingworth, had worked their way up the table with some inspired captaincy from Tom Moody. In the previous match against Northants on a last-day turner, he had bowled more than 30 overs of unaccustomed off-spin to take five for 148. Tim Curtis was called in to bowl 11 overs of leg breaks, dismissed Kevin Curran, and Worcestershire won the game.

Phil Weston had been in the runs for Worcestershire with a double century against Northants and a hundred against us, but it was having Graeme Hick around all summer that was the major boost for them. England had decided that they could do without him in their top six and so Hick could concentrate on hammering county bowlers. I think we might have offered him 65 and 31 before our game and felt relieved to have been let off lightly. In the past he has murdered us – 252 not out and 100 not out at Abergavenny in 1990, 219 not out at Neath in 1986. At his best, he is quite capable of destroying any bowling attack. He has scored over 90 centuries and he is still only 31. In his early years, his foot movement and balance, allied to his confidence, were exceptional. Not too many Glamorgan bowlers queued up to bowl at him. The 1991 West Indians and the unenviable label of England's new 'Messiah' were too much to handle all at once. But he has few peers in the county game.

Mike Powell came in to replace Tony Cottey, the vice-captain, in Glamorgan's top six. Cottey had not been in form with only two 50s all season – and one of those was against Oxford University. Powell scored his unbeaten double century in the same match and, with six other hundreds for the second team, had forced his way in and deserved his chance. Alun Evans was another who was pushing for a place. He had bags of potential but his first-team opportunities had been limited.

Mike was undoubtedly looking for more than a pair on his county championship début. It was not the most auspicious of débuts but it demonstrates that it is a huge step up to first-class cricket in this country. We definitely need a more competitive league structure to ease the climb to the top.

It was a weekend for meeting old friends and visitors. Some of my schoolfriends from Blundell's had come up to Worcester to watch. They saw little of me at the wicket but it was very pleasant to meet up with some characters that I had not seen since I left school in 1982.

Micky Stewart came over too. He wanted to discuss my application for the job at Lord's. The disappointment at my lack of runs at New Road was temporarily forgotten as he informed me that I was on the shortlist along with a few other applicants. I was surprised and delighted to have made it so far. Now, I would have to prepare for an interview at the end of the season. Could it possibly be my last month as a first-class cricketer? It was a frightening prospect. The job was a tremendous challenge. It was also a great opportunity and I was sure that I wanted it.

Trying to keep it confidential was going to be so difficult. Cricket is a small world and rumours spread quickly. I decided that I would tell Debbi and my parents. I did not want the media to add pressure by speculating about whether it would be my last season or not. Nor did I want to disrupt the team before the end of the season.

I had to lie to Duncan Fletcher when he asked me about Micky Stewart's visit. I said we had been discussing the ECB's staff assessments of the candidates for senior coaching positions. We had been talking about that, but so much else besides.

It is inevitable in a game like cricket that comparisons will be made between players of the past and present. Such discussions have been going on since the game began. Was Grace a better batsman than Hobbs? Was Bradman the best of the lot? The record books say he was and that is all that any player can do – beat the records set by those in the past. The changing face of first-class cricket means that the records of the all-time greats are unlikely to be approached, however. Single-innings records are within reach as Brian Lara has proved. But the aggregates of

Hobbs and Woolley, the 197 centuries of Hobbs, the 4,187 wickets of Rhodes and 1,649 dismissals of Taylor are never to be eclipsed because we do not play enough first-class cricket.

Graeme Hick will some time next season score his 100th first-class century. His current ratio of hundreds to innings played is over one in six. Hobbs scored hundreds at one in four and played until he was over 50 to reach 197. If Hick is to beat Jack Hobbs' record then it will take him at least another 20 years and, keen and fit as Graeme is, I do not expect to see him batting at New Road when he is 52.

Yet the fascination with comparisons continues. In the *Glamorgan Yearbook* for 1997, the journalist Paul Rees suggested that there were similarities between the 1969 championship-winning team and Glamorgan in 1997. 'Where there was Jones, there is Morris; for Lewis read Maynard; for the all-rounder Walker there is Croft; and while Shepherd was an off-cutter and prolific wicket-taker, Watkin is one of the most consistent seamers on the circuit.' Watty was certainly proud to be compared with Shep, and being closely identified with Alan Jones was a real compliment to me. But even comparisons of style are not appropriate. The game has changed so much, even since I have been involved at first-class level. Every player is fitter than ever before, the bowling is more accurate and varied than in the early 1980s and there are still enough speed merchants around to unsettle opening batsmen. The surprise is that while the game over here has improved in certain aspects, abroad the improvement has been even more startling. The real comparison is not between then and now, it is between them and us.

Worcestershire 1st innings

Curtis			b	Croft	160
Weston			lbw	Butcher	17
Hick	c	Maynard	b	Croft	65
Haynes	c	Shaw	b	Waqar	45
Moody			lbw	Butcher	42
Sheriyar		ret hurt			2
Leatherdale	c	Morris	b	Butcher	23
Solanki	c	Maynard	b	Croft	8
Rhodes	c	Morris	b	Thomas	33
Lampitt			c & b	Thomas	49

Mirza	not out		1
Extras			31
Total: 9 wkts dec 146.3 overs			476

Fall: 1-34, 2-212, 3-295, 4-337, 5-365, 6-378, 7-397, 8-459, 9-476

	O	M	R	W
Waqar	25	7	86	1
Watkin	33	11	82	0
Butcher	20	4	87	3
Thomas	21.3	1	92	2
Croft	39	11	80	3
Dale	8	1	30	0

Glamorgan 1st innings

James	c	Rhodes	b	Haynes	69
Morris	c	Solanki	b	Sheriyar	4
Dale			b	Haynes	9
Powell	st	Rhodes	b	Haynes	0
Maynard		not out			161
Butcher	c	Solanki	b	Lampitt	5
Shaw			lbw	Mirza	15
Croft			c&b	Leatherdale	27
Thomas			b	Lampitt	25
Waqar	c	Weston	b	Mirza	46
Watkin	c	Lampitt	b	Mirza	1
Extras					36
Total: all out 68.4 overs					398

Fall: 1-43, 2-72, 3-78, 4-107, 5-124, 6-155, 7-218, 8-294, 9-394

	O	M	R	W
Sheriyar	11	3	72	1
Mirza	17.4	1	95	3
Haynes	11	1	46	3
Lampitt	11	0	82	0
Hick	5	0	27	0
Leatherdale	10	0	55	1
Moody	3	1	9	0

Worcestershire 2nd innings

Curtis	c	Shaw	b	Watkin	11
Weston	c	Shaw	b	Croft	114
Hick	c	Dale	b	Croft	31
Haynes			lbw	Watkin	33
Moody	c	Thomas	b	Croft	14
Leatherdale			lbw	Waqar	2

Solanki	c	Powell	b	Croft	5
Rhodes	c	Shaw	b	Waqar	27
Lampitt		not out			18
Mirza		run out			0
Sheriyar	c	Croft	b	Waqar	9
Extras					31

Total: all out 104.5 overs   295

Fall: 1-13, 2-69, 3-130, 4-159, 5-161, 6-174, 7-249, 8-277, 9-278

	O	M	R	W
Waqar	20.5	6	50	3
Watkin	24	7	49	2
Thomas	11	1	38	0
Butcher	6	1	44	0
Croft	42	10	98	4
Powell	1	0	3	0

Glamorgan 2nd innings

James	c	Curtis	b	Leatherdale	130
Morris		run out			37
Dale	c	Lampitt	b	Moody	13
Powell	c	Solanki	b	Haynes	0
Maynard	c	Rhodes	b	Haynes	0
Croft	c	Lampitt	b	Mirza	33
Butcher			c&b	Moody	18
Shaw		run out			5
Waqar		not out			44
Thomas			lbw	Mirza	1
Watkin	c	Lampitt	b	Mirza	0
Extras					30

Total: all out 76.3 overs   319

Fall: 1-115, 2-135, 3-152, 4-152, 5-230, 6-269, 7-269, 8-300, 9-309

	O	M	R	W
Sheriyar	6	2	12	0
Mirza	13.3	1	53	3
Hick	12	3	38	0
Moody	22	3	105	2
Lampitt	5	0	36	0
Haynes	12	1	34	2
Leatherdale	6	0	23	1

FIFTEEN

In the Country

Glamorgan v Northamptonshire
Abergavenny, 20–23 August 1997
Britannic Assurance County Championship

		P	Pts
1.	GLOUCESTERSHIRE	13	181
2.	KENT	12	171
3.	GLAMORGAN	12	165
4.	WORCESTERSHIRE	12	159
5.	SURREY	13	153
6.	MIDDLESEX	12	149
7.	YORKSHIRE	12	148
8.	ESSEX	12	147
9.	LANCASHIRE	13	141
10.	WARWICKSHIRE	12	137
11.	LEICESTERSHIRE	13	132
12.	SOMERSET	12	128
13.	NOTTINGHAMSHIRE	12	125
14.	HAMPSHIRE	13	116
15.	NORTHAMPTONSHIRE	12	104
16.	DURHAM	12	98
17.	SUSSEX	13	96
18.	DERBYSHIRE	12	95

At last – Abergavenny. A beautiful but small ground in a magnificent setting under Sugar Loaf Mountain on the edge of the

135

Brecon Beacons. It's been a batsman's delight for the most part with its flat pitch and short boundaries. I played in the first county championship match to be staged on the ground in 1983, against Worcestershire, who have been fairly regular visitors to the Pen-Y-Pound ever since. Graeme Hick had slaughtered our bowling in the 1990 match – 252 not out and 100 not out – as Watty, of all people, went for 202 off his 42 overs. Hick was spectacular then, but five years later Gloucestershire turned up with a young man named Andrew Symonds who had raised a few eyebrows around the circuit by smashing county attacks everywhere in his début season at the tender age of 19. At 79 for five, Gloucestershire were in danger of following on, but that became merely academic as he hit whatever was bowled at him far and wide. His 254 not out contained 16 sixes – a world record – the last three disappearing into the crowd behind the long-suffering bowler, Steve Watkin. So Watty has no reason to remember Abergavenny fondly, but over the years I had enjoyed myself there, with a total of nine 50s and two centuries. If there was anywhere that was likely to help me put my season back on track, it had to be Abergavenny.

Northamptonshire did not have the fearsome attack they had possessed in the past. No Curtly Ambrose, no Anil Kumble and they were languishing towards the bottom of the table. This had not been one of our 'must wins' at the start of the season, but in the light of missing out against Hampshire and Notts, it was a late addition to the list. We were all too well aware, though, that gaining a positive result on such a fine batting track could be at the whim of the captains. Northants may not be blessed with bowling of great impact, but they had three batsmen who could hit hard and often for a long time – Rob Bailey, Kevin Curran and David Sales, who, in 1996, became the youngest player to score a double century in a championship game. Our bowling line-up was back at full strength with Dean Cosker having been released by the Under-19s. Unfortunately the batting line-up was depleted when I twisted my ankle having collided with Darren Thomas when playing touch rugby on the outfield before the game. That meant a hurried call to Alun Evans who was with the 'Twos' at Lensbury where they were about to play Middlesex.

Physio Dean Conway took one look at my ankle, ruled me out of the match and suggested that my bones had the texture of poppadums. So Evans drove back 150 miles to make his first championship appearance of the season and only his ninth in first-class cricket. With Mike Powell still keeping Tony Cottey out of the side, the batting had a curious look about it. If I was to be elsewhere in 1998, the two youngsters had a chance to stake an early claim for a place. And where better for a batter than Abergavenny?

The match had barely begun when everyone was looking rather quizzically at the pitch. When the creases were measured it was found that the popping and return creases were five inches out of alignment. After half an hour's delay, play resumed with Roberts and Warren facing Waqar and Watkin.

Northants' 330 was no better than par on Pen-Y-Pound and it might have been worse but for Kevin Curran who made 159 – never timing it properly but taking full advantage of some unusually slack Glamorgan fielding. Once again the reply was led by Steve James. Opening with Alun Evans, he was able to encourage his young partner while playing his own game. Mike Powell, on his home ground, played sensibly along with Matthew Maynard and, once again, maximum bonus points had been picked up inside 90 overs. At 61 for five, Northants seemed to have no chance of making a game of it but Sales and David Ripley stayed together to the close of the third day, with Sales becoming more and more belligerent and looking a fine prospect.

With so much unsettled weather around, Glamorgan's immediate task on the Saturday morning was to remove Sales before too much damage was done and the chance of victory disappeared.

In the absence of Maynard – off the field with a dislocated finger – and with neither myself nor vice-captain Cottey playing, it was Waqar who skippered the team. He opened not with himself on the last morning, but with Watty and Cosker. When Waqar did bring himself on, Sales hoisted him for six to reach 99. That was about the end of any substantial resistance. Waqar shot out the tail, five wickets going for 27, and it was down to whether we could make 196 off 71 overs. The captain was unlikely to bat and Evans had ricked his back. Yet again we depended on Jamer and he did not disappoint. Well as Curran and Sales had played, Steve looked a class above anybody else in this game. How England could continue to ignore him was becoming an ever-louder subject of discussion around the ground and subsequently in the press. His 15th 50 in 22 innings duly arrived, followed by his third century in succession. There were black clouds looming over the Beacons, and drizzle held up play for a while, but with it tipping down virtually everywhere else in South Wales, the clouds somehow skirted Abergavenny and the target was reached in the 50th over with Powell, appropriately on his home patch, hitting the winning runs. A full house – 24 points, and for a while we were top of the table.

Gloucestershire were not involved in this round of matches but Kent were, over at Taunton. Driving back home, the sports pro-grammes on the radio were more concerned with Manchester United being held to a goalless draw at Leicester and Llanelli going down at Bridgend 22–21. Eventually we discovered that Kent needed 161 in 26 overs and, with Alan Wells going well, they were on course. The next we heard it was a draw with the scores level so Kent picked up 16 points. We were top by two points with four more games to play – but three of those were away from home. Injuries appeared to be stacking up too – Maynard's finger, Evans's back, and Dale was carrying a back injury too – but Cottey and I were ready to go again. Robert Croft also had something to prove. A year before, he had been capped for England for the first time against Pakistan. Twelve months on, England had dropped him, he had been fined for his part in the ridiculous incident at Chelmsford and had then received a suspended ban from the Nat West trophy. He seemed genuinely bewildered by the media attention – especially when it was high up the running order of *News at Ten* on the night *after* the incident. He was also hurt that much of the criticism of his performance in the Test matches suggested that he was not trying hard enough to eradicate his problem against the quick bowlers. 'How can they ever question my effort for the team?' he asked. Crofty was too much of a character to be down for long. In any case he had an important part to play for Glamorgan as the season built up to a climax.

Like many other people, I offered to help Robert work his

way out of the problems he was experiencing against the quicks. I had also been in the firing line of fast bowlers at Test level and I felt that the lessons I had learned from my experiences of playing Ambrose, Walsh, Marshall and Patterson at the Oval in 1991 might be of use to him. The most important thing, though, was to choose one person to work with, so that suggestions and advice are not conflicting from different sources. With Graham Gooch so heavily involved with England it was right that Robert did a 'John Morris' and sought Gooch's advice.

We needed Croft to be back at his best, Jamer to keep firing and the rest of us providing the support. Waqar had taken ten wickets in the match at Abergavenny, and nobody could have hoped that he would have managed that on such a batting track. Steve James was just unstoppable. He had surely done enough to earn a place on England's tour of the Caribbean. It was not as if he was likely to be overawed by the prospect or feel out of place. Mike Atherton he knew well from his Cambridge University days – in fact, Mike was due to be an usher at Steve's wedding at the end of the season. Perhaps there had been too much talk about the Steve James of the old days, scoring all his runs through third man. He had changed significantly since then.

Glamorgan's chairman, David Morgan, has played a major part in taking the county forwards. He was also a great help and loyal supporter throughout my career. When I relinquished the captaincy in 1989 at Bristol, David was vice-chairman to Tony Lewis. He accepted my resignation but was quick to stress that it should only be a temporary measure as he wanted to see me back in charge.

In some difficult times, David would be the one that I would turn to as some of the others in authority had a tendency to criticise rather than help. David usually came out with sound advice.

Some of the players think I am a wine buff. I am not really – I just enjoy drinking it! David, however, is something of a connoisseur with a well-stocked and impressive cellar which I have enjoyed on several occasions.

When I applied for the job of Technical Director I felt that it was appropriate to let David know of my ambitions. He was extremely supportive. He has risen through the ranks at Lord's and is chairman of the First-Class Forum and deputy to Lord MacLaurin. He was a leading figure in the transition of the TCCB/NCCA to ECB and has played a key role in mapping out Glamorgan's future – particularly in building and developing the ground at Sophia Gardens. Glamorgan is very fortunate to have a man of his ability and keenness around at just the right time.

Northamptonshire 1st innings

Roberts			lbw	Waqar	14
Warren	c	Shaw	b	Watkin	4
Fordham	c	Maynard	b	Thomas	22
Bailey	c	James	b	Croft	20
Curran			b	Croft	159
Sales	c	Maynard	b	Waqar	22
Ripley	c	Shaw	b	Waqar	5
Taylor	c	Shaw	b	Croft	28
Akram		run out			22
Davies			lbw	Waqar	17
Brown		not out			8
Extras					9
Total: all out 106.2 overs					330

Fall: 1-18, 2-18, 3-51, 4-123, 5-176, 6-182, 7-261, 8-298, 9-302

	O	M	R	W
Waqar	22.2	6	78	4
Watkin	22	6	49	1
Croft	28	5	68	3
Thomas	15	1	80	1
Dale	4	0	17	0
Cosker	15	5	31	0

Glamorgan 1st innings

James		run out			103
Evans	c	Curran	b	Davies	31
Dale	c	Bailey	b	Brown	71
Thomas	c	Bailey	b	Davies	19
Powell		not out			41
Maynard	c	Fordham	b	Bailey	58
Croft	c	Fordham	b	Bailey	15
Extras					16
Total: 6 wkts dec 89.2 overs					354

DNB: Shaw, Waqar, Watkin, Cosker

Fall: 1-84, 2-200, 3-232, 4-246, 5-332, 6-354

	O	M	R	W
Akram	12	1	57	0
Taylor	13	1	49	0
Curran	9	4	17	0
Davies	29	5	109	2
Brown	24	3	90	1
Bailey	2.2	0	18	2

Northamptonshire 2nd innings

Warren	c	Maynard	b	Waqar	12
Roberts	c	Cosker	b	Watkin	11
Fordham	c	Evans	b	Watkin	25
Bailey	c	Shaw	b	Waqar	2
Curran	c	James	b	Waqar	2
Sales	c	sub	b	Waqar	103
Ripley			lbw	Croft	58
Taylor	c	Shaw	b	Waqar	0
Akram	c	Waqar	b	Croft	1
Davies		not out			1
Brown			b	Waqar	0
Extras					4

Total: all out 79.2 overs 219

Fall: 1-24, 2-31, 3-33, 4-35, 5-61, 6-192, 7-193, 8-198, 9-219

	O	M	R	W
Waqar	22.2	4	56	6
Watkin	21	6	41	2
Croft	21	5	54	2
Thomas	4	0	24	0
Cosker	11	4	40	0

Glamorgan 2nd innings

James	c		lbw	Brown	113
Shaw	c	Bailey	b	Brown	11
Dale	c	Warren	b	Davies	36
Waqar	c	Brown	b	Davies	9
Powell		not out			10
Croft		not out			8
Extras					10

Total: 4 wkts 48.1 overs 197

Fall: 1-40, 2-163, 3-179, 4-183

	O	M	R	W
Akram	11	2	46	0
Taylor	6	0	21	0
Brown	18	3	68	2
Davies	13.1	0	59	2

SIXTEEN

Tears for the Princess

Leicestershire v Glamorgan
Grace Road, 27–30 August 1997
Britannic Assurance County Championship

		P	Pts
1.	GLAMORGAN	13	189
2.	KENT	13	187
3.	GLOUCESTERSHIRE	13	181
4.	YORKSHIRE	13	170
5.	WORCESTERSHIRE	13	169
6.	MIDDLESEX	13	158
7.	ESSEX	13	155
8.	SURREY	13	153
9.	LEICESTERSHIRE	14	152
10.	WARWICKSHIRE	13	144
11.	LANCASHIRE	13	141
12.	SOMERSET	13	139
13.	NOTTINGHAMSHIRE	13	134
14.	HAMPSHIRE	13	116
15.	NORTHAMPTONSHIRE	13	109
16.	DURHAM	13	108
17.	DERBYSHIRE	13	103
18.	SUSSEX	14	100

Just my luck! Missing out on Abergavenny meant that the next
chance to rehabilitate the Morris batting was at Grace Road, a

county ground that has improved significantly over the years and which is now very well appointed, but I still could not bring myself to like playing there. Maybe this is because I never made runs at Grace Road – but then I did not score too many at Worcester and that was one of my favourite grounds. There is no logic to it, a player either feels that he can play on a certain ground or he cannot. At Grace Road I just did not feel comfortable. By contrast, Jamer was delighted to be back. In 1995 he had scored 230 not out there – then the best post-war individual score by a Glamorgan batsman. More of the same would do us nicely, and Steve too, as Graham Gooch had come up to watch him. The weather was the crucial factor, though: another unsettled forecast, plenty of rain likely and the prospect of us having to do everything in double-quick time if we were to salvage a few points.

Not that it was likely to be easy against Leicestershire, the reigning champions. They may not have won very many matches, but the weather was having even more of a say in their season than it was in ours. Beating Leicestershire was obviously a difficult proposition; in their championship-winning year they lost just once – at the Oval. In 1997 they were beaten for the first time just a couple of weeks before they met us – oddly enough, at Eastbourne – where, in a game of forfeits, Sussex won for the first time. Forfeits looked a distinct possibility when rain forced the abandonment of the first day's play at Grace Road.

So on the Wednesday evening we were in good time for the start of the game at Filbert Street, watching Leicester against Arsenal. This was a rare treat for the Gunners fan in our ranks – the man who was born in South Africa, brought up in Chepstow but still has an affiliation for a team from north London – Adrian Dale. How can I scoff? Me, a Liverpool fan. The match ended in a 3-3 draw, a last-minute cliff-hanger, with Daley so delighted that he forgot that he was in the middle of the Leicester supporters and celebrated after Bergkamp's hat-trick as though he was standing on the old North Bank at Highbury.

Grace Road, Day Two. We did play, but it was not much fun. Steve went, caught behind off David Millns. As Graham Gooch had been joined by David Graveney, presumably to see if Steve was tour material, it was an unfortunate time to end a run of three successive centuries. I was trying my best to underline that I was far from a spent force when Millns produced a ball that pitched leg and middle and hit the top of the off stump. I thought it was all but unplayable – a few in the press-box agreed. We staggered on to 180 for seven against two of Leicestershire's young discoveries, James Ormond and Dominic Williamson. Williamson was making his championship début; 21 years old from Durham, he seemed an aggressive character whose medium-fast bowling will only quicken up in the next few years as he develops.

Croft and Waqar took us beyond 200 on the Friday morning when we were happy to settle for whatever we could glean off a miserly Leicestershire attack. Then it all suddenly came right for Watty. Throughout the season he had been valuable support for Waqar but he was starting to wonder whether he would ever take five wickets in an innings again. His career-best eight for 59 was taken at Edgbaston in 1988. It had been two years since he returned six for 55 against Yorkshire at Bradford but he was back at his best at Grace Road: in-swingers, out-swingers, slower balls, they all worked even to the extent of providing me with a couple of catches at slip and a first-innings lead that looked most unlikely 24 hours earlier.

In the quest to regain some sort of form I had all but forgotten that I was close to scoring a thousand runs for the season. I needed 34 at the start of our second innings. Steve went for 21 to young Williamson who again displayed his aggressive nature by hurling some abuse at the nation's top run-scorer when he edged to first slip.

Dale and Powell were also out before bad light brought proceedings to a premature halt. I still needed another 11 for my thousand. I was lucky to have survived. I top-edged a hook off Ormond that was not caught. He was bowling quickly, a shade below Waqar's pace, and, like Williamson, is an aggressive character. Waqar earlier in the day had struck him for a huge six over extra cover, which prompted a few words from Ormond. It certainly did not faze Waqar but there were more than a few old heads nodding in appreciation of a fast bowler who is not likely to be put off his sole intention – bowling fast to take wickets.

The following morning we arrived at Grace Road to find there was no chance of play. The groundstaff had decided after hearing a weather forecast that gave no hint of rain that only the pitch should be covered and not the full square. In the event, it had rained for six hours and the ground was saturated. The umpires Barry Dudleston and Dickie Bird had no option but to abandon the game. Dickie could make a trip across the East Midlands to watch his beloved Barnsley play at Derby County. That was of little compensation for him, I think he loves cricket so much.

The umpires would be making a report to Lord's and we intended to complain too but there was little that could be done about it. Leicestershire themselves were embarrassed but blamed it on the high water table. They insisted that even if they had covered the whole square we still would not have been able to play.

In the meantime the news came through that Yorkshire had been rained off at Old Trafford when they were poised for a win that would have taken them into contention for the title. David Byas blamed inadequate covering at Old Trafford. We had fallen foul of that too, in the Sunday League game in June, the covers had been used at Aigburth and when it rained in Manchester there were not enough left to do the job properly.

We played football on the outfield at Grace Road, then retired to the dressing-room. Gloucestershire appeared likely to start against Notts at Bristol and a win there would put them clear at the top. Kent's match at Hampshire seemed unlikely to bring a result. A few of us decided to go to Welford Road to watch Leicester Tigers. The conversation was full of 'if onlys'. On the radio, the Little Fireman was promising there would be no easy points for Gloucestershire.

Gloucester RFC gave Leicester a run at Welford Road. Leicester's star line-up included Back, Healey, Johnson and Stransky and they won in the end 33–16. After the match, we heard that Wales had beaten Romania by a decent margin at Wrexham and that Gloucestershire looked like winning against Notts.

Information was not easy to obtain on Gloucestershire's progress. Ceefax did not seem to work on the hotel television. The radio gave us Gloucestershire needing a hundred off 15 overs with Alleyne and Russell batting. 'They'll get those,' was the unanimous verdict of Glamorgan. We were resigned to being equal second in the table with Kent.

The next report told us Russell had gone (cheers) but Ball had hit Evans for six (gloom again). That left 32 wanted off five overs. ('Easy, run a ball,' the Glamorgan expert commented.)

We tuned in half an hour later expecting to hear confirmation that Gloucestershire had cantered home. Remarkably, the collapse had continued and they had been bowled out for 239, 22 runs short. The Little Fireman had kept his promise even to the extent of declaring before he had completed his first century of the summer. 'Told you they'd do it,' came the voice of Glamorgan cricket.

We were joint top of the table with Kent with three games to play and I was not on Sunday League duty the following day. The best method of celebrating seemed to be for Watkin and Morris to locate the best balti in Leicester, retire early and sleep long into the following morning.

Breakfast in the Grand Hotel, Leicester, on Sunday, 31 August. Everyone says that you never forget where you were when you hear news that makes history.

I had beaten Steve to the bathroom and then to the breakfast table. Cereal and orange juice. He walked straight over to me, his eyes wide, staring.

'What's the matter?' I asked him.

'Princess Di,' he replied. 'She's dead. Killed in a car crash in Paris.'

For a few seconds nobody said a word. I looked around. How many of the team had met her when she came to our Centenary Match against Gloucestershire in 1987? As captain I had been given the honour of presenting the team to her – Jamer, Matthew, Cotts and I were the only ones left. John Hopkins, Geoff Holmes, Greg Thomas, Colin Metson, Corrie Van Zyl, Steve Barwick and Steve Monkhouse had been the others.

I found myself thinking of the photograph my mother had framed of Prince Charles and Princess Di in our team line-up. They were both turning to me. What had she said? I could hear her voice: 'Are you growing that moustache for a bet?'

The royal couple had attended that game because she was patron of Gloucestershire and Prince Charles of course was patron of Glamorgan. Before the game she told our then secretary, 'Your boys are in for a real beating today!' She was right – we lost by seven wickets. It was a gloriously hot sunny day. What a contrast with that grey Sunday in Leicester.

Glamorgan 1st innings

James	c	Nixon	b	Millns	14
Morris			b	Millns	8
Dale			lbw	Wells	69
Powell	c	Nixon	b	Ormond	3
Maynard			b	Ormond	0
Cottey	c	Nixon	b	Williamson	25
Shaw			b	Williamson	0
Croft	c	Wells	b	Williamson	35
Waqar	c	Sutcliffe	b	Wells	28
Watkin	c	Nixon	b	Millns	1
Cosker		not out			1
Extras					42
Total: all out 57.5 overs					226

Fall: 1-32, 2-33, 3-65, 4-71, 5-126, 6-126, 7-159, 8-205, 9-216

	O	M	R	W
Millns	16	3	58	3
Ormond	15	4	64	2
Pierson	5	0	23	0
Williamson	9.5	3	19	3
Wells	12	2	52	2

Leicestershire 1st innings

Wells	c	Shaw	b	Watkin	3
Maddy	c	Shaw	b	Waqar	20
Sutcliffe			b	Watkin	19
Whitaker			lbw	Croft	62
Johnson			b	Watkin	6
Smith			b	Watkin	0
Nixon		not out			47
Millns			b	Watkin	1
Williamson			b	Watkin	3
Ormond	c	Morris	b	Watkin	7
Pierson	c	Morris	b	Watkin	2
Extras					5
Total: all out 62.4 overs					175

Fall: 1-7, 2-39, 3-62, 4-78, 5-78, 6-135, 7-141, 8-145, 9-167

	O	M	R	W
Waqar	13	3	53	1
Watkin	19.4	6	41	7
Dale	3	0	23	0
Croft	16	5	35	2
Cosker	11	5	18	0

Glamorgan 2nd innings

James	c	Johnson	b	Williamson	21
Morris		not out			23
Dale			b	Wells	13
Powell			lbw	Wells	0
Cottey		not out			6
Extras					4
Total: 3 wkts 24.2 overs					67

Fall: 1-35, 2-61, 3-61

	O	M	R	W
Millns	6	2	20	0
Williamson	8	2	21	1
Ormond	6	3	16	0
Wells	4	1	8	2
Maddy	0.2	0	0	0

SEVENTEEN

The War of Words

Surrey v Glamorgan
Foster's Oval, 2–5 September 1997
Britannic Assurance County Championship

		P	Pts
1.	KENT	14	197
2.	GLAMORGAN	14	197
3.	GLOUCESTERSHIRE	14	187
4.	YORKSHIRE	14	180
5.	MIDDLESEX	14	178
6.	SURREY	14	177
7.	WORCESTERSHIRE	14	175
8.	WARWICKSHIRE	14	165
9.	ESSEX	14	159
10.	LEICESTERSHIRE	15	159
11.	NOTTINGHAMSHIRE	14	156
12.	LANCASHIRE	14	150
13.	SOMERSET	14	148
14.	HAMPSHIRE	14	125
15.	DURHAM	14	119
16.	NORTHAMPTONSHIRE	14	115
17.	DERBYSHIRE	14	111
18.	SUSSEX	15	103

From Leicester we went straight to London for the game against
Surrey at the Oval. We were due to start on Tuesday because of

the Nat West final on the Saturday. What a week to be in London. It was impossible to comprehend the outpouring of grief that affected the whole country. Everyone appeared to be in a state of shock. Even London became a quieter, more polite place that week. The small things were most noticeable, like other drivers letting you out at road junctions, no jostling on the tube and people saying sorry.

By the end of the week that did not apply to events inside the Oval. Going into the game there were 20 points covering the top six sides. In sixth place were Surrey; a full set of points against us and they would be right in there challenging for the title. Of their last three games, two were against title contenders – Glamorgan and Kent – and the other was against Lancashire whom they would confidently expect to beat.

Darren Thomas led the call for us all to have a daffodil and 'Champions '97' tattooed on our backsides if we won the title. The old-stagers tried to decline politely and derision from the rest of the team was instantly heaped on James, Watkin and Morris.

Surrey looked likely to parade their full array of England stars against us: Butcher, Stewart, Thorpe, the Hollioakes, Ally Brown plus the bowlers Bicknell, Benjamin, Salisbury and their overseas spinner Saqlain. On paper they are the strongest side in the championship, but England calls and a penchant for pressing the self-destruct button has meant that they have underachieved in recent years.

They do make it difficult for themselves, but then other counties love to beat Surrey. At least one goes so far as to impose fines on any team member who is seen shaking hands with a Surrey player. Had they started the season in the kind of form they produced from July onwards, they would have won the title by a country mile.

Team selection posed a problem for Glamorgan at the Oval. Mike Powell had been promised 'a trot' in the first team by Matthew Maynard. How long is a trot? In his three games he had scores of 0, 0, 41*, 10*, 3 and 0. I thought that four games was a 'trot' but he was replaced after three and Tony Cottey was back. It was a difficult one to balance: Surrey at the Oval, a good batting track, but very good bowlers – a championship battle with all the tension that entails. It would have been an experience for Powell, but too early an experience?

It was interesting to see Waqar back at the Oval where he made his name. Several of his former colleagues were still in residence and Waqar wanted to demonstrate that he had not made a mistake by refusing their offer of a re-engagement at the end of last season.

My incentive was obvious – a century against the old 'Brown Hats' to complete my full set against all the counties.

Our bowling performance on the first day was either the best of the season or very close to it. Waqar, Watty, Thomas and Croft all on top form, Adrian Shaw took five catches behind the stumps and Surrey just topped 200.

Then Surrey bowled excellently at us. Jamer started in his usual fashion before he was LBW. I touched one from Saqlain to Alec Stewart. The innings was revived by Dale and Maynard. Cottey, Croft and Thomas kept it going – an impressive knock from Thomas particularly. He had taken three wickets, then he hit 75 not out. It was the season in which he undoubtedly matured as a cricketer.

On the Thursday morning we were bowled out for 438, a reasonable lead especially if we could remove a few of them early. Stewart, Butcher and Ratcliffe had duly gone by the time they had scored 32. Thorpe and Brown pulled it round for Surrey till we had a lucky break. Thorpe's drive was deflected on to the stumps by Cosker and Brown was run out. With luck like that it was definitely going our way.

Both Hollioakes came in and attacked, however, and by the end of the day Surrey were 90 ahead with four wickets left, though crucially one was Graham Thorpe, 140 not out, having played superbly under intense pressure throughout. There was absolutely no doubt in my mind that he had proved himself to be the best batsman in the country by that innings.

The next day he went on to 222. A career best, he had played Surrey right back into the game. We were left requiring 254 off 46 overs. We decided to have a go early on but at 65 for three we were not making progress. Matthew decided to call it off and we all agreed. To have played as we did at Worcester and lost would have enabled Surrey to close right up in the title race. As it was, they were now effectively out of it and we were still in it, just.

It was then that the row blew up. Surrey accused Matthew of being 'unenterprising'. I can think of several words to describe Matthew but 'unenterprising' is not one of them. Dave Gilbert, the Surrey coach, launched an astonishing attack: 'It was outrageous that they should have given up so early. It had the makings of a great game. If that's the way they think they can win the championship, they can't expect any favours from us when we play Kent in the final game'.

He went further, adding: 'If there's any justice then Kent will win the title because they are the best all-round side. They are prepared to lose games in order to win them.'

Duncan said very little at the time, but it was obvious that he was very angry about Dave Gilbert describing Kent as the strongest team in the country – before Surrey had even played them. At the end of the season Duncan expressed his disappointment with Gilbert's comments: 'There were only two games where I would accept that we were outplayed – Derbyshire and Middlesex. Against Middlesex it only went wrong after we'd done well for the first two days. We defeated Kent with a lot to spare. Unlike some counties, we are a team that plays with our hearts, not with our mouths!'

There is little doubt in my mind that Surrey were more disappointed with themselves than with Glamorgan. Their title challenge had started late, and it was all the more impressive for that, but they left themselves with too much to do. By ensuring a draw, we narrowed down the championship contenders and ruled them out of the race. If the positions had been reversed I am sure they would have done the same thing. Matthew was convinced he had taken the right option: 'We didn't have a chance of winning. The pitch was wearing; they had two world-class spinners (Salisbury and Saqlain), a draw was our best option.'

Debbi had come up from Cardiff and, as we drove across London to her parents' place that Friday evening, it struck me that if it was to be my last season in first-class cricket, I would be retiring without the full set of centuries. I set myself another target – to retire with a title. A future without county cricket still seemed so unlikely to me. I had managed to keep my application for Micky Stewart's job a secret. I had told only my immediate family and a couple of close friends. I knew from the shortlist – John Barclay, Martyn Moxon, Kim Barnett and Phil Neale – that I had only an outside chance of being appointed but I also knew it was the only job I would leave county cricket for. Whatever came about in the following few weeks was certain to contain an element of sadness. If I did have only two weeks left as a professional cricketer then I wanted there to be no disappointment at the end of it all. I had been in the game too long and seen too many of the lows to finish anywhere but at the top.

That evening we joined the crowds who had made their way into Central London and who were walking quietly but purposefully towards Kensington Palace. The scent of millions of flowers was hanging in the air. People were talking in murmurs. There was a pervading sadness in everyone who was there. We laid a small bunch of flowers among the vast number of tributes already in place.

Surrey 1st innings

Butcher			lbw	Watkin	20
Stewart	c	Shaw	b	Waqar	6
Ratcliffe	c	Morris	b	Croft	9
Thorpe	c	Shaw	b	Thomas	13
Brown	c	Shaw	b	Watkin	60
A. Hollioake			lbw	Croft	22
B. Hollioake			lbw	Croft	14
Saqlain	c	Shaw	b	Thomas	21
Bicknell	c	James	b	Waqar	17
Salisbury		not out			8
Benjamin	c	Shaw	b	Thomas	3
Extras					11
Total: all out 71.2 overs					204

Fall: 1-11, 2-36, 3-49, 4-60, 5-96, 6-138, 7-154, 8-186, 9-196

	O	M	R	W
Waqar	16	3	55	2
Watkin	16	6	42	2

Thomas	11.2	3	36	3
Croft	23	5	54	3
Cosker	5	1	14	0

Glamorgan 1st innings

James			lbw	Bicknell	23
Morris	c	Stewart	b	Saqlain	16
Dale	c	Stewart	b	B. Hollioake	72
Maynard			c&b	Bicknell	76
Cottey	c	Stewart	b	B. Hollioake	34
Croft			lbw	B. Hollioake	53
Shaw			lbw	Salisbury	8
Thomas		not out			75
Waqar	c	Butcher	b	Saqlain	15
Watkin			lbw	A. Hollioake	19
Cosker			lbw	A. Hollioake	0
Extras					47
Total: all out 115 overs					438

Fall: 1-30, 2-50, 3-172, 4-229, 5-264, 6-305 7-337, 8-366, 9-438

	O	M	R	W
Bicknell	30	4	93	2
Benjamin	13	0	72	0
Saqlain	31	8	96	2
B. Hollioake	25	3	91	3
A. Hollioake	2	0	12	2
Salisbury	14	1	51	1

Surrey 2nd innings

Butcher	c	Cosker	b	Watkin	7
Stewart	c	Shaw	b	Waqar	2
Ratcliffe	c	Cottey	b	Croft	14
Thorpe	c	Watkin	b	Cosker	222
Brown		run out			41
A. Hollioake			lbw	Waqar	65
B. Hollioake			b	Thomas	31
Saqlain	c	Morris	b	Croft	17
Bicknell	st	Shaw	b	Cosker	53
Salisbury	c	Cottey	b	Cosker	14
Benjamin		not out			1
Extras					20
Total: all out 129.4 overs					487

Fall: 1-5, 2-9, 3-32, 4-95, 5-215, 6-264, 7-337, 8-366, 9-438

	O	M	R	W
Waqar	23	4	79	2
Watkin	22	1	78	1
Croft	37	4	128	2
Cosker	23.4	2	107	3
Thomas	24	3	79	1

Glamorgan 2nd innings

James	c	Stewart	b	Salisbury	28
Morris	c	Stewart	b	Bicknell	9
Shaw		not out			36
Croft	c	A. Hollioake	b	Salisbury	7
Maynard		not out			26
Extras					1

Total: 3 wkts 32 overs   107

Fall: 1–21, 2–55, 3–65

	O	M	R	W
Bicknell	11	1	32	1
Benjamin	4	0	22	0
Saqlain	5	0	19	0
Salisbury	11	2	31	2
A. Hollioake	1	0	2	0

EIGHTEEN

Rocky II

Glamorgan v Essex
Sophia Gardens, 10–13 September 1997
Britannic Assurance County Championship

		P	Pts
1.	KENT	15	220
2.	GLAMORGAN	15	208
3.	YORKSHIRE	15	202
4.	GLOUCESTERSHIRE	15	193
5.	WARWICKSHIRE	15	188
6.	MIDDLESEX	15	186
7.	SURREY	15	185
8.	WORCESTERSHIRE	15	180
9.	ESSEX	15	179
10.	NOTTINGHAMSHIRE	15	163
11.	LEICESTERSHIRE	15	159
12.	SOMERSET	15	156
13.	LANCASHIRE	15	154
14.	NORTHAMPTONSHIRE	15	138
15.	HAMPSHIRE	15	134
16.	DURHAM	15	122
17.	DERBYSHIRE	15	115
18.	SUSSEX	15	103

Not everyone shared our view that we had done the right thing by opting for a draw at The Oval and so ensuring that Surrey would not be a factor in the final run in. Yorkshire had beaten Worcestershire by 66 runs at Headingley which meant Worcestershire were out of it, but Yorkshire were only six points behind us and they had to play Kent at Headingley next. Kent themselves meanwhile had taken Gloucestershire apart and were top of the table, 12 points clear with their destiny in their own hands. If they won against both Yorkshire and Surrey then there was nothing we could do about it.

If we had won at The Oval, our critics argued, we would have been a point clear. A big 'if'. To play:

10-13.9.97	Cardiff	Glamorgan v Essex
	Edgbaston	Warwickshire v Gloucestershire
	Headingley	Yorkshire v Kent
18-20.9.97	Derby	Derbyshire v Yorkshire
	Canterbury	Kent v Surrey
	Taunton	Somerset v Glamorgan

The game with Essex at Cardiff was dubbed 'Round Two' after the Ilott-Croft confrontation at Chelmsford. The repercussions of that incident had rumbled on for so long everywhere, except the Glamorgan dressing-room, meaning that there was never any likelihood of a repeat. Essex were playing for pride and talent money – fourth place was not out of their reach. Having come more or less fresh from winning the Nat West Trophy at Lord's and putting to rest the black memories of the year before, Essex were thought likely to have no inhibitions and play their usual brand of attacking cricket.

In the lead up to the game, the media in Wales was re-running the finale to the 1969 season. The penultimate game of the season was Essex at Swansea when Glamorgan won by running out John Lever off the last possible ball. We would settle for that again but hoped to wrap it up a little earlier if at all possible.

Steve James was out for two. It typified a rotten week for him as he had failed to make the England team for the Caribbean. Instead he was picked as vice-captain for the 'A' team to Kenya and Sri Lanka. He had played well enough to leave nobody in any doubt about his capabilities. He deserved to go to the West Indies – nobody could have done more – and it was no surprise that there was a certain amount of reaction to his disappointment, but the mini-bad patch he went through towards the end of the season was a mere blip, his first bad run for two years.

Somehow I rediscovered a semblance of form and battled through to 82. That was a lot more like it but some still way from my best. Even so, I was disappointed not to reach three figures on what was possibly my last appearance at Sophia Gardens. We secured the four batting points as we reached 361.

We lost 27 overs due to bad light on the second day. We were becoming fatalistic about the time that we had given up to the weather during the season. As long as we were on the field at some stage of the day, we were delighted. We could not afford any more complete days sitting in the pavilion watching the rain pour down.

Once again there was an inspired bowling performance from Waqar and Watty. Essex were all out for 169, even though Stuart Law played quite superbly, hitting 55 off 63 balls. Watching him, I could not understand why he had failed to make the Australian team. One correspondent the following morning compared him with Bradman – 'beautifully balanced', according to Christopher Martin-Jenkins in the *Daily Telegraph*. 'Tight defence or irresistible attack.' Despite his fine innings, Essex followed on.

Meanwhile, at Headingley, Kent took a first-innings lead over Yorkshire as Steve Marsh, with a captain's innings of 84, ensured that 172 runs were added for the last three wickets. They were still 12 points ahead of us.

Essex made a much better fist of it in their second innings, though Law only made nine. Half-centuries from Prichard, Hussain, Irani and Grayson kept the third successive decent crowd at Sophia Gardens waiting and worrying. Irani opened up to hit Waqar back over his head for four. Waqar took this personally – a gesture of disrespect – went up a gear and bowled as quickly as at any time in the summer.

Watty took five wickets in the innings when he polished off the tail on the fourth morning. He was back in wicket-taking mode at just the right time: 149 was all we needed to bank 24 precious points.

Even so, there were jitters in the dressing-room. I was pleased to be heading out to the middle where at least I could do something other than watch. Caught at the wicket off Cowan for a duck was not at all in the scheme of things. Disgruntled, I trudged off for possibly the last time at Cardiff and joined the others on the balcony.

We sank to 26 for three with hopes depending on Matthew. Somebody had to show some real discipline and it was the captain and the vice-captain who came through. The crowd were not going to allow us to let this one slip. They roared and cheered every run as the necessary total came closer. Matthew was batting as responsibly as I had ever seen him. Mission was accomplished to good effect, with Yorkshire and Kent scrapping out a draw. Kent appeared to be in real trouble with Chris Silverwood taking five wickets, but an unbeaten half-century from Matthew Fleming and some stout defending from Mark Ealham kept Yorkshire out as the weather closed in.

Darren Thomas was delighted to be given his county cap at tea on the last day at Cardiff – he was nearing 50 wickets for the season and it was fully deserved for his much improved play and attitude during the year.

A point clear and one match to go. A win at Taunton with maximum bonus points and there was nothing anybody could do to stop us. The dressing-room mood was surprisingly quiet. We would have liked to have got started against Somerset right away. All we wanted to do was go to Taunton and finish the job.

Like most counties, Glamorgan have a number of regular supporters who follow the team almost everywhere there is a game. Few of the regulars are as keen or as knowledgeable as Fred Raffle.

Fred was born in Northumberland. In early childhood he lost his sight and went to the College for the Blind in Worcester. It was there by playing cricket and going down to New Road that he developed his interest in the game. At school he and his friends adopted counties. Worcestershire was not allowed to be chosen – it was the county of the 'prison'. Being a Northumbrian, Yorkshire was not an option, so Fred settled for the county of his best friend, who lived in Cardiff, and began taking an interest in Glamorgan in the days of McConnon, Parkhouse, Watkins and Wooller.

Between 1958 and 1960 he studied for his Diploma in Social Science at Swansea University. After lectures he and a group of friends would walk past St Helen's and drop in if there was a game in progress. His friends would commentate on the action for him and, inevitably, with Shep on his way to his second thousand, the afternoons would be full of Shep taking barrowloads of wickets. In 1959 they went up to the Arms Park to see the Indian tourists against Glamorgan, hoping for another good performance from Shep to earn him a place in the England side. 'Just like these days,' says Fred, 'we would wait, huddled around the radio, for the announcer to read out the 12 for the next Test. We usually waited in vain for a Glamorgan name. Shep should have been in, but never was.'

Shep was Fred's hero, but by the time he moved on to Durham University to complete his degree, he had only 'heard' Shep, never met him. His fascination with cricket continued. The radio, with its ball-by-ball commentaries, was a godsend, especially in winter when the early-morning commentaries from Australia would crackle the news of the latest Ashes series. 'I doubt if I've missed a commentary from Australia since they started. From the days when we used to listen "illegally" under the bedclothes at school to people like the great John Arlott. I've always wanted to be close to the people who talk and write about the game.'

But Fred's career took him away from Wales and the county game. For ten years he taught blind children in Surrey, not missing the chance to introduce them to cricket. He started an Old Boys' Cricket Club from his old school in Worcester and, after only two years, there were 180 blind cricketers playing on a regular basis in the south of England.

In 1972 he moved back up north, taking a job with Sunderland Borough Council working across the range of social services from child care to mental health. Fred was determined to prove to himself and everyone else that blind people can function and take responsibility for others in society. Cricket had to take a back seat, but his interest never waned.

By 1982 he was in Nottingham working on rehabilitation programmes for newly blind people. To his delight he found that he was only a short walk from Trent Bridge and took the opportunity to drop in from time to time, meeting amongst others Dickie Bird, Derek Randall and Mike Hendrick.

Fred had played for England at blind cricket, he had rowed and water-skied too, so it was inevitable that he would not be able to stay away from sport and cricket in particular for long.

Six years later, he was in Birmingham as head of the Specialist Rehabilitation Unit for the Blind at the National Mobility Centre. Fred was responsible for the training of teachers for the blind, aiming to bring in a new approach – psychological rather than mechanical. Previously, the attitude to helping blind people was 'give them a white stick and they can go from A to B'. Fred was more interested in helping them want to go from A to B in the first place – then the white stick had a purpose. He was instrumental in ensuring that the college was absorbed into the University of Central England. Having struggled for funding and to keep within budget, the centre became part of mainstream education and Fred was principal of the Department of Rehabilitation until 1993.

His job involved checking the progress of student teachers when they were sent on their initial placements. In 1990 one of his students was in Brighton and Fred was there to report on the way he was approaching his new job. That night he sat in the bar of the Dudley Hotel having just heard on the radio that Viv Richards had made a century off 73 balls against Sussex, just down the road in Hove.

Across the other side of the bar, the BBC Wales commentator Edward Bevan rose from his seat to buy his colleague Don Shepherd a drink. As he ordered, Fred looked up and said, 'Those are fine South Walian tones, what are you doing here?', hoping that it might have something to do with the cricket and then he could find out more about Viv's innings. Bev explained and a conversation developed. Fred mentioned his years at Swansea when he followed Glamorgan and said that his great hero was

Don Shepherd. 'You're not going to believe this,' said Bev, 'but this drink I've just bought is for him.' From then on Fred has been a fixture on the county circuit wherever Glamorgan have been playing. In fact he has been to every county headquarters when Glamorgan have been playing – except Trent Bridge, strangely enough. Bev, Shep and their scorer Andrew Hignell have welcomed him into their box. Andrew and Fred and the guide dog Ivar frequently room together on away trips.

Ivar is a character himself. Fred's original golden labrador was retired and replaced by a black labrador named Ivor. In honour of Viv Richards that was soon changed to Ivar. Viv, no animal lover, did not know what to make of it, but he once acknowledged to Fred that Ivar would be better than the other one – 'because he's black!' Ivar is often to be seen in the company of Matthew Maynard or any one of the Glamorgan players, being taken for a walk round the boundary.

Fred loves cricket and the atmosphere of the game. 'I enjoy the camaraderie. I've known some players for seven years now and we've never had a cross word. They've never suggested I'm a nuisance. They always help me pour a drink or hand me a plate of food. They are first rate. They will always come up to me, pat my arm and say who they are.'

In recent years Fred has become even more adventurous. Thanks to Barry Dudleston's tour company, he has been able to go abroad to support England in South Africa, Zimbabwe and New Zealand. He went to the Hong Kong Sixes at the end of the season and plans a trip to Sharjah and then the West Indies. It was in Zimbabwe that he met Jack Russell. Jack was not a part of England's Test plans but he said that meeting Fred put all his problems into perspective. To have been with Fred for any length of time and seen his love of the game and his determination not to be at all handicapped by his blindness is a lesson for all of us.

Ivar is not too keen on Fred's absences to watch cricket abroad. He is a bright, intelligent and gentle dog, capable of being shown a room in an unfamiliar hotel once and then knowing his way back there without fail hours later. Andrew Hignell recalled one night in Leeds, walking back from the pub to the hotel with Fred and Ivar; a pack of loose dogs were barking and playing further up the road. Andrew and Fred were neatly rounded up by Ivar and firmly moved in the opposite direction.

On Fred's return from New Zealand, he took Ivar out for his first walk and suddenly found himself being directed into a hedge. As he struggled to haul himself out of the branches, Fred swears that Ivar was laughing, Mutley-style, his harness and lead rattling as if he was saying: 'That'll teach you to go away without me, you old blighter!'

During the Essex game at Sophia Gardens, the Glamorgan total reached 111 for three. According to cricketing superstition, feet must be lifted off the floor until a run is scored otherwise it is bad luck. Edward Bevan, in the middle of his commentary, was surprised to look around and see Shep, Fred and Watty all with their feet off the floor and Watty holding a startled Ivar in his arms.

Glamorgan 1st innings

James	c	Robinson	b	Ilott	2
Morris			lbw	Ilott	82
Dale			b	Ilott	49
Maynard			c&b	D. Law	71
Cottey	c	Prichard	b	D. Law	46
Croft	c	Hussain	b	Grayson	16
Shaw	c	Cowan	b	Grayson	6
Thomas			b	D. Law	39
Waqar	c	S. Law	b	D. Law	17
Watkin		run out			3
Cosker		not out			0
Extras					30
Total All out 119.4 overs					361

Fall: 1-8, 2-146, 3-149, 4-276, 5-277, 6-286, 7-301, 8-337, 9-356

	O	M	R	W
Ilott	22	4	65	3
Cowan	5	1	26	0
D. Law	24.4	6	69	4
Grayson	33	7	84	2
Such	31	6	82	0
S. Law	4	0	16	0

Essex 1st innings

Prichard	c	James	b	Waqar	6
Robinson	c	Shaw	b	Watkin	12
Hussain	c	Cottey	b	Waqar	0
S. Law	c	Dale	b	Watkin	85
Irani			lbw	Thomas	7
Grayson			lbw	Thomas	0
D. Law	c	Morris	b	Watkin	15
Hyam		run out			10
Ilott		not out			26
Cowan			b	Waqar	0
Such	c	sub	b	Croft	0
Extras					8
Total: all out 43.2 overs					169

Fall: 1-6, 2-6, 3-70, 4-79, 5-79, 6-122, 7-133, 8-156, 9-156

	O	M	R	W
Waqar	11	2	31	3
Watkin	14	2	68	3
Croft	8.2	2	10	1
Thomas	8	0	48	2
Cosker	2	1	4	0

Essex 2nd innings

Prichard	c	James	b	Croft	51
Robinson	c	Maynard	b	Watkin	0
Hussain			b	Watkin	53
S. Law	c	Shaw	b	Watkin	9
Irani			b	Waqar	50
Grayson		not out			98
D. Law			b	Waqar	1
Hyam			lbw	Thomas	26
Ilott			b	Croft	7
Cowan	c	Shaw	b	Watkin	13
Such	c	Croft	b	Watkin	5
Extras					27
Total: all out 100 overs					340

Fall: 1-2, 2-104, 3-123, 4-130, 5-211, 6-215, 7-277, 8-292, 9-320

	O	M	R	W
Waqar	22	2	82	2
Watkin	26.4	9	68	5
Croft	31	6	86	2
Cosker	11	3	25	0
Thomas	18	0	54	1

Glamorgan 2nd innings

James			b	Cowan	4
Morris	c	Hyam	b	Cowan	0
Dale			b	Such	12
Maynard		not out			75
Cottey		not out			35
Extras					24
Total: 3 wkts 44.1 overs					150

Fall: 1-4, 2-13, 3-26

	O	M	R	W
Ilott	13.1	2	43	0
Cowan	11	4	14	2
Such	12	2	35	1
D. Law	4	0	19	0
Grayson	4	0	23	0

NINETEEN

Eleven to Win

Somerset v Glamorgan
Taunton, 18–20 September 1997
Britannic Assurance County Championship

		P	Pts
1.	GLAMORGAN	16	232
2.	KENT	16	231
3.	WARWICKSHIRE	16	212
4.	YORKSHIRE	16	212
5.	MIDDLESEX	16	209
6.	WORCESTERSHIRE	16	204
7.	GLOUCESTERSHIRE	16	197
8.	SURREY	16	188
9.	ESSEX	16	183
10.	LANCASHIRE	16	178
11.	SOMERSET	16	177
12.	LEICESTERSHIRE	16	170
13.	NOTTINGHAMSHIRE	16	166
14.	HAMPSHIRE	16	155
15.	NORTHAMPTONSHIRE	16	147
16.	DURHAM	16	127
17.	DERBYSHIRE	16	117
18.	SUSSEX	16	107

There had surely never been a week like it in cricketing history in Wales. In 1969 the title was won at home with a match to spare. The thrilling climax this time was already playing on the nerves of the sporting public in Wales before we had even left Sophia Gardens for Taunton.

It was also the week of the vote for a National Assembly. There was very little doubt in the minds of the people I spoke to that the game at Taunton was far more important, though when one chap asked me, 'What are you going to do?' I told him that I thought we would win but that it would be a struggle. Not the answer he was looking for – he was referring to the vote.

There were further rumbles of controversy up London way when Surrey decided to rest Graham Thorpe for the game against Kent. Their team was beginning to look very depleted. No Thorpe, Adam Hollioake was injured, and Martin Bicknell and Chris Lewis were affected by injuries too. With Saqlain already away with Pakistan, Surrey were asked for an assurance that their attitude to the match would be beyond reproach. The Surrey chief executive gave such an assurance to the ECB and that was the end of the matter. In the end, Chris Lewis did play and it was Kent who, without Martin McCague, Dean Headley and Paul Strang, were probably the more under strength of the two.

The weather forecast was worrying as we arrived in Taunton after an afternoon's practice at Sophia Gardens, so too was the fact that Waqar was complaining of a stomach upset. With a man of his experience it was unlikely to be a simple case of nerves. Waqar had played in all 15 matches since he came over to join us – some achievement.

The number of Glamorgan supporters who had made their way across the Severn Bridge was quite astonishing. We would not lack for support. In many ways it was reminiscent of Canterbury '93. That was only for one day – would they all have the stamina to party and cheer for four whole days?

It was decided that the best method of winning the game would be to put Somerset in if we won the toss. We had studied the pattern of games at Taunton over the season and to bat last, it appeared, would give us the best chance, especially as Mushtaq Ahmed was ruled out with injury.

Matthew did the business and Waqar, though far from well,

took out Holloway's off stump, then induced Ecclestone to edge to me at slip. It came like a tracer bullet, but somehow my hands held it in front of my throat. Self-protection, most likely.

Waqar had to leave the field for a while which was of some concern, especially as Somerset flourished in his absence with Turner and Lathwell looking comfortable until Turner hooked Watkin to fine leg. Trescothick was well caught by Matthew at cover and 113 for four was looking promising for us. After lunch Waqar came back. Lathwell was dropped, then bowled by Waqar. Burns followed, but Bowler held the fort till Watty found the edge. We had the bowling points in the bag. The first objective had been achieved.

Batting against Caddick was not much fun as the light closed in. He trapped Jamer leg before, then removed Daley. I would have gone too but the edge to slip was not held. It was then that Matthew began to play with resounding authority. He overtook me in no time at all and just purred on to his 50 off 43 balls. It was a supporting role for me and I was quite content to watch him unleash shot after shot. Ben Trott, making his début in place of Mushtaq, was treated with utter disdain – his first two overs cost 21. If it is any consolation to him, not everyone in county cricket can play like Maynard.

Overnight we were 159 for two with Matthew 76 not out while I had reached 49.

On the second morning the rain just persisted out of a slate-grey sky. There seemed little chance of a start. Then, after three, it became a little brighter, the rain stopped and amazingly we were under way before four. At Canterbury, Kent had bowled Surrey out for 124 so we had to assume that nothing less than a win and maximum points would be good enough for us to take the title.

We had to forget about the bad light and the drizzle. Attack was the only way of playing the game. At the wicket, Matthew started as he had finished on the previous evening with a flurry of scintillating strokes that propelled the total beyond 250. In nine deliveries from Caddick and Shine we hit eight boundaries between us. Maynard had softened them up, I was cashing in. I have never seen such a devastating display – even Viv Richards could not have matched it. The most outstanding feature of his innings was that it was played in such adverse conditions, under the pressure of knowing that, if he got out, the new batsman would be facing a near-impossible task. As it was, when Matthew was caught at slip for a quite breathtaking 142, we had put on 235 at virtually a run a ball. He had faced just 116 balls and was applauded off the field by everyone, including some much relieved Somerset bowlers who had suffered from his unbelievably clinical yet powerful assault.

Along with the help of Cottey and Croft, I stayed there until we had made the fourth batting point. There were five lights on the board, it was the darkest that I had ever played first-class cricket in and I immediately appealed against the light when we reached 353 for four off 68 overs. It had been a fantastic achievement, which would have been exceptional in good light on a warm midsummer day. It went a long way towards putting us in an impregnable position. Even though I was there I look at the scorecard now and wonder 'How on earth?'.

Over at Canterbury the Pitches Advisory Panel had warned Kent for preparing a wicket that was not suitable for the start of a four-day match. With Kent only making 220 in their first innings, we had a little breathing space; but, as a result there looked certain, we could not afford to relax our grip at Taunton. Alec Stewart and Darren Bicknell had put Surrey back in the match – but Kent were still the more likely winners.

I came off the field that Friday evening and later met a few members of the national press in an impromptu conference in the pavilion. I was delighted at having made a big hundred. Did not know quite what to make of the Welsh Assembly. No, I had never played cricket at this level in the dark before. Matthew's innings had been superb. Croft and Cottey had done brilliantly to come in and stay there. And what? 'Is this your last game for Glamorgan?' 'Why?' 'Because you are on the shortlist for the Technical Director's job at Lord's.' How the press came to hear of it I shall never know. I had told very few people and only those I trusted. I had sworn them to secrecy. I had not told any of the team. That was something I had to do immediately.

I must admit that I did play that innings at Taunton as though it was my last for the club. I wanted to play a central role in a crucial win. I had not been in form at all towards the end of the season and I really wanted to contribute something substantial at the end.

I told the players at the team meeting that Friday night that it could have been my last game for the club. Some were genuinely shocked by the news. All of them wished me well. I thought it was important they heard it from me that I was up for the job at Lord's and didn't find out from reading the papers. It was a simple courtesy to the team, some of whom I had played with and been friends with for a decade and more. I think Watty was a little surprised that I had managed to keep it a secret from him for so long. When we had travelled so much together and spent so much time in each other's company, it was remarkable that I had succeeded in not giving him, or any of the others, an inkling.

The following morning Crofty and I went out to the wicket. It appeared that the Welsh had occupied Taunton – the first invasion since the referendum? I was as relaxed as I have ever been for an important innings. I felt good about it too; usually a trace of nerves is good for me, it aids concentration. Duncan had done a fine job of putting us in the right frame of mind. The instructions on that Saturday morning were simple – 'get as many as you can, as fast as you can'. The weather was still likely to be a factor, and if possible we wanted a finish that day.

We set off quite merrily. I had taken my score to 165 when Caddick sneaked one through, just when my thoughts were turning towards 200. With Croft and Shaw carrying on in attacking vein, 174 runs were added in 30 overs, which gave us a distinctly workable lead of 275.

Waqar, for once, just could not pitch it right. Turner in particular took a liking to his full length. Darren Thomas was brought on first change and he bowled as fast as at any time in his career so far – in the slips we were standing back further for him than for Waqar. He took his 50th wicket of the season but Somerset were not about to fold and give us the game. Lathwell made runs again, but when we thought that we were through to the tail, Caddick and Rose combined to add 95 in 14 overs. Rose was in one of his most belligerent moods and in the end was unlucky to be given out caught behind when it probably came off his thigh pad.

Eleven to win. There was no chance of it being one of those occasions when the regular openers allow a couple of tail-enders to knock off the runs, even though the celebrations were starting in the dressing-room. Watty asked me to grab a stump for him at the end. The necessary runs were acquired in a not totally convincing fashion. As Steve glanced the winning boundary, I reached for the stumps, then had a sudden thought, 'Had we made enough?' I looked at the scoreboard with my arms full of stumps and wondered whether I should put them back in. The crowd coming over the boundary boards told me that I had not made a complete fool of myself.

'Champions!' – a long-term ambition achieved. My last act as a first-class player was to dash off the field, screeching with delight and sheer elation.

The dressing-room was packed with people, most of whom I had never seen before in my life. They could have been committee, press, members, officials. Everybody, it seemed, wanted to be a part of a fantastic achievement. Microphones were appearing but very little sense was being spoken into them. Outside the crowd was starting to sing. Crofty led them in a verse or two of 'Alouette' for some reason best known to himself. The kit was vanishing out of the dressing-room at an alarming rate. Watty was given his stump, while I managed to hide the other two. Somebody mentioned that Kent had won so that we were four points clear at the finish. Four points, one point – it mattered not a jot. The achievement was all that counted and how we had done it. It was a triumph for team spirit, masterly planning and no little ability.

We had a 'subdued' celebration afterwards. The overwhelming sensation was not one of sheer exultation, more a really pleasant weariness and relief that it had all worked out so well. The adrenaline rush of the moment of victory lasts so briefly. Within hours the actions become history.

We left Taunton to the remaining supporters who could not bear to leave the scene of the great Welsh victory. By Sunday lunchtime I was in the local in Cowbridge. J.P.R. Williams came over to say, 'Congratulations! It was so gripping, I couldn't turn over the TV to watch the rugby!'

The following morning we went to Bristol Airport to fly to Greece for a family holiday. It was strange retracing the route some of the way back to Taunton. I was sure some of the traffic coming the opposite way over the bridge was bringing home the last few Glamorgan fans who could now boast once again that their county were the champions.

Relaxing on the beach with Debbi, Bethan and Emily, I wondered whether it was really the last time I would play in county cricket. It seemed so unlikely after 17 years.

On my return it all happened so quickly. Two interviews at the ECB and all of a sudden I was being offered the job. 'Think about it,' said Tim Lamb. No doubt he understood what a wrench it would be for me to leave Glamorgan, especially after that last season. The thinking was already done, though. I had told myself that this was the job I wanted. It was the only job I would give up playing for. I accepted.

Somerset 1st innings

Turner	c	Thomas	b	Watkin	40
Holloway			b	Waqar	0
Ecclestone	c	Morris	b	Waqar	0
Lathwell			b	Waqar	62
Trescothick	c	Maynard	b	Croft	20
Burns			b	Waqar	28
Bowler	c	Morris	b	Watkin	63
Rose			lbw	Cosker	13
Caddick	c	Croft	b	Cosker	11
Shine	c	Morris	b	Watkin	6
Trott		not out			1
Extras					8
Total: all out 68.4 overs					252

Fall: 1-17, 2-17, 3-72, 4-113, 5-155, 6-156, 7-197, 8-217, 9-251

	O	M	R	W
Waqar	12	3	41	4
Watkin	13.4	2	61	3
Thomas	16	2	53	0
Cosker	14	3	42	2
Croft	13	1	49	1

Glamorgan 1st Innings

James			lbw	Caddick	8
Morris			b	Caddick	165
Dale	c	Bowler	b	Caddick	8
Maynard	c	Bowler	b	Shine	142
Cottey	c	Bowler	b	Shine	13
Croft			lbw	Rose	86
Shaw		not out			53
Thomas	c	Ecclestone	b	Trott	0
Waqar	c	Ecclestone	b	Trott	5
Watkin	c	Shine	b	Trott	5
Cosker			b	Caddick	7
Extras					35
Total All out 99.4 overs					527

Fall: 1-12, 2-42, 3-277, 4-293, 5-404, 6-475, 7-476, 8-482, 9-495

	O	M	R	W
Caddick	34.4	5	132	4
Shine	17	3	88	2
Rose	29	3	152	1
Trott	11	0	74	3
Burns	7	0	65	0
Bowler	1	0	9	0

Somerset 2nd innings

Turner			b	Thomas	38
Holloway	c	Shaw	b	Thomas	25
Ecclestone	c	Morris	b	Watkin	10
Lathwell			b	Thomas	47
Trescothick	c	James	b	Croft	16
Burns	c	Shaw	b	Thomas	18
Bowler			lbw	Thomas	3
Rose	c	Shaw	b	Watkin	67
Caddick		not out			56
Shine	c	James	b	Watkin	0
Trott			lbw	Cosker	0
Extras					5
Total: all out 70.4 overs					285

Fall: 1-60, 2-67, 3-88, 4-133, 5-145, 6-153, 7-166, 8-261, 9-273

	O	M	R	W
Waqar	11	0	84	0
Watkin	15	1	75	3
Thomas	15	2	38	5
Cosker	11.4	3	34	1
Croft	18	5	51	1

Glamorgan 2nd innings

James	not out	9
Morris	not out	1
Extras		1
Total: 0 wkt 1.2 overs		11

	O	M	R	W
Caddick	1	0	5	0
Rose	0.2	0	5	0

TWENTY

And in the End

		P	W	L	D	Bt	Bo	Pt
1.	GLAMORGAN	17	8	2	7	50	57	256
2.	KENT	17	8	4	5	44	60	252
3.	WORCESTERSHIRE	17	6	3	8	49	54	228
4.	MIDDLESEX	17	7	4	6	33	56	219
5.	WARWICKSHIRE	17	7	2	8	32	51	219
6.	YORKSHIRE	17	6	3	8	41	54	215
7.	GLOUCESTERSHIRE	17	6	6	5	35	60	206
8.	SURREY	17	5	5	7	39	52	192
9.	ESSEX	17	5	6	6	39	55	192
10.	LEICESTERSHIRE	17	4	1	12	37	54	191
11.	LANCASHIRE	17	5	6	6	34	54	186
12.	SOMERSET	17	3	3	11	38	64	183
13.	NOTTINGHAMSHIRE	17	4	3	10	26	55	175
14.	HAMPSHIRE	17	3	5	9	42	41	158
15.	NORTHAMPTONSHIRE	17	3	5	9	33	48	156
16.	DERBYSHIRE	17	2	9	6	32	59	141
17.	DURHAM	17	2	8	7	22	56	131
18.	SUSSEX	17	1	10	6	24	57	115

It finished so abruptly. One minute we were all together on the balcony of the pavilion at Taunton, and then, all too soon, we were going our separate ways. Me, I suppose, most of all. I missed out on the parade through Cardiff because I was away on holiday. When the team was presented to the crowd at the Cardiff-Llanelli match at the Arms Park, I was enjoying a celebration meal with my parents and the rest of my family the day before I moved to London. It seemed that, no sooner had I decided to move on from Glamorgan, the cord was cut.

Starting at Lord's with all that 'optimistic trepidation' I had experienced before the start of a new season or a big game, I knew it was a mammoth job that I was taking on. In the few quiet moments, I found myself thinking of joining up with the rest of the team for the presentation of the trophy by the Duke of Edinburgh at Buckingham Palace in mid-November. We had had little time together to savour the triumph, and now perhaps there would be one last gathering of us all. Yet I should have realised that the last and only time we would all be together would be on that balcony at Taunton. I was already, in my own mind at least, a 'former Glamorgan player'. Matthew was away in New Zealand, captaining England in the Cricket Max series. Waqar was in Pakistan, ready for the arrival of the West Indians. Duncan was coming back from South Africa for the occasion but there were still some doubts about whether he would be with Glamorgan for another tilt at the title.

In fact we were not 'all together' on the Taunton balcony as Gary Butcher, who had played in nine of the championship matches, was not there. He had intended to go down to Somerset on the Sunday, but when the wickets began to fall he decided to set off on the Saturday afternoon in the club car lent to him by Darren Thomas. Unfortunately, it had an immobiliser fitted. Gary could not work out how to start it and had to settle for watching us clinch the title on television. He did not have much luck with cars in 1997.

Colin Metson did make his way to Taunton and was on the balcony at the end. He had come with a bootload of bats for us all to sign so that he could auction them at his remaining benefit functions. It was becoming obvious that the parting of the ways was inevitable and, shortly afterwards, he announced his retire-ment – forced out, he felt, as 'I often found the situation frustrating and at times a little bizarre'. He thought that there were times during the season when he should have been stumping and not Adrian Shaw.

Matthew Maynard took the decision to play Adrian Shaw and the management team, myself included, supported that decision. I thought it was a brave decision and the right one. Matthew wanted more runs from the lower order, which meant that Shaw was the best option and he wanted support for the team ethic, which left him no choice.

Shawsy has spent most of his life in and around dressing-rooms of various kinds – notably as a centre for Neath. He is a team man, extremely fit and dedicated to improving his game; he knows the areas he has to work on. In the media, especially locally in Wales, he received harsh treatment from those who were demanding the return of Metson as wicketkeeper. He felt that he had to play twice as well at home as away because he was being scrutinised and often pre-judged by those who did not understand the reasons for dropping Metson. As a result, Shaw was frequently far more nervous than he should have been at home and it was only through continued reassurance from Matthew that he settled into the role and became an integral and valued member of the team. In my opinion, he was the right man for the job.

At his best, Colin was a top-class wicketkeeper, but it was he himself who pointed out that 'a cricketer today needs to be good at two out of three things – batting, bowling and fielding. If a batsman can field, there is no need for him to bowl.' But a keeper does not have the bowling option and he must be able to hold his own as a batsman. If he had thought back to our pre-season sessions with the psychologists, he might have added a few more attributes to being a success – pulling together being one of them. That was where Adrian Shaw scored most convincingly over Colin Metson.

I will certainly say to every wicketkeeper that I see making his way up in the game that it isn't good enough anymore to be a brilliant stumper with no other aspect to your game. If you want to reach the top, then you will have to be a decent batsman. Then again, I would say to any potential opening batsman, always be looking to develop other facets of your game, as most good batsmen have the capability to be safe catchers close to the wicket. To a quick bowler I would advise improving the batting technique – it will always be valuable for the team and the team is all-important.

I hate to remind Glamorgan supporters of the improvement in the batting of Peter Such. He is only averaging about seven now, but in 1990, when he joined Essex, it was only two! Of course he is not a batsman but his improved confidence with the bat undoubtedly resulted in him being able to hit Darren Thomas through the covers for four in that tense Nat West semi-final at Chelmsford.

The more one player has to offer is important. That does not mean we have to lose character and individuality. I understand why people love Devon Malcolm when he comes in to bat because they never know whether he will score nought or ten in the first two balls. That makes great entertainment but, having seen Robert Croft working hard to improve his technique against short-pitched deliveries from quick bowlers, I know that we cannot afford to be cavalier in our approach to the game.

Australia, South Africa, the West Indies and Pakistan have found ways of producing better all-round cricketers than we have. The finished article is ready far earlier through their systems than through ours. Now, given Micky Stewart's approach to the development of young players, we can be more optimistic. I have to continue the progress made by Micky and produce a structure for English cricket that ensures we have the best team in the world. I want Australia and South Africa and the rest to look at us and see the way ahead.

At the end of the season, Mike Powell was named the Second-XI Player of the Year by the England and Wales Cricket Board (before I arrived there, so there was no Glamorgan influence from me). He scored 1,210 runs in the Second-XI champion-ship, including five centuries, and he made that 200 not out on his début in first-class cricket. He is a rare talent and he is still only 20. It is up to people like me to see that he, in racing parlance, 'trains on'.

I am under no illusions. It is an enormous job ahead. I have a huge remit to improve coaching and playing standards from the playground to the Test ground. Players like Mike Powell must not get lost *en route*. Technically, a youngster may be very good, but stepping up to first-class level is different and difficult. Mike has found that, but he must come again next season, whoever coaches him. Coaches do not have a high enough profile even though they have such an important role to play.

Even if you have the ability to play at first-class level, you still need other professional skills, like goal-setting, motivation and concentration in order to succeed. Coaches need to be equipped to pass these on to the next generation. The system itself has to be right, which is where the premier leagues come in.

None of this is meant to stifle dreams or restrict personality or character. Cricket must have its Hammonds and Huttons, Truemans and Bothams. Part of my job is to make sure that when talent is discovered it stays with cricket and matures to its full potential.

Even before I arrived at Lord's I was mocked in the Welsh press for using 'management-speak'. Terms like 'goal-setting, motivation and concentration' were dismissed as 'flabberjabber'. But it is not just jargon. Having worked with youngsters for the past few years, I have been surprised at the number of those with real talent who have no idea how to harness it. Look at some of the gifted cricketers who have appeared for England in the last decade, try to match their achievements with their ability and it is obvious that many have fallen short. Mark Ramprakash is an obvious case in point, but previously Keith Fletcher, Graham Gooch and Mike Gatting all needed more than 50 Test innings before they made a century. Geoff Miller failed to score a first-class hundred until his 380th innings – 12 years after his début. Yet, when it all fell into place, each one of them looked a different player. We have to ensure that our young players are able to take each step towards Test level with confidence and that, once there, like the Australians, they are not overawed.

I am with the late Carwyn James, the coach of the 1971 British Lions team which went to New Zealand and won the series when he wrote (about rugby but it applies equally to cricket) that it 'is first and foremost about attitudes. Unless the approach is right, the basics and the skills will suffer and no values of any dimension, least of all aesthetic, will be achieved.'

For myself, I think I can say that I always tried to play within the traditions of cricket and will always be aware of the glorious history that provides so much of the fabric of the game. I will try to pass that on.

When I walked through the Grace Gates for the first time as an ex-player, on 3 November 1997, I could look back on not a bad season. I did not achieve all the targets I set myself, only 1,207 runs instead of 1,500. However, I am fourth on the Glamorgan all-time run-scorers list, until Matthew overtakes me. Records are there to be broken. Alan Jones set standards for others to aspire to and records for others to achieve. I hope that I have done the same.

Nor do I have a full set of hundreds to take into retirement as I failed to manage one against Surrey. And I only made four 100s in 1997 instead of six as I had hoped. We did not reach a one-day final but I did improve my career best to 233 not out.

In my last first-class match I scored a century – 165 – and it took a current England bowler to get me out. To do that in my last season proves that I can still play a bit and I will continue to do so – whenever I can.

Regrets? None. Except perhaps that I was not born a fast bowler. I would have liked just one season as a genuine out-and-out tearaway quickie, sprinting in down the hill at Headingley, bouncing them out at the Oval, taking a hundred wickets in a season and going on tour to Australia, running in at the SCG . . . well, perhaps not.

Just now I am content that, at the end of it all, I went to Lord's with a title.

And finally, when it became widely known that I was taking the job at Lord's, various letters, cards, faxes and phone calls were made to me, mainly from players I had met over the years on the county circuit. The gist of the messages was that, if I was retiring, they suddenly felt old! One in particular came from Kent:

As one who has done a not inconsiderable amount to boost your career statistics, I am ecstatic about your retirement. Many congratulations on a truly fantastic, if unrecognised and unrewarded, career. What a fantastic way for you to bow out – county champions – enabling us to be the top English county! The very best of luck pushing all that paper around your desk.

'Jazzer' Fleming.

APPENDIX ONE

Glamorgan's three championship-winning sides – 1948, 1969 and 1997 – a comparison by statistics

1948 – P.26, W.13, L.5, D.6, ND.2

	M	I	NO	Runs	HS	Avge
Jones (W.E.)	26	40	6	1425	212*	41.91
Davies (E.)	26	42	1	1636	215	39.90
Parkhouse	26	40	1	1141	117	29.25
Dyson	6	8	1	202	51	28.25
Wooller	25	36	5	775	89	25.00
Watkins	22	35	4	765	101	24.67
Muncer	25	34	7	581	67*	21.51
Clift	23	37	1	725	73	20.13
Eaglestone	24	36	4	595	72	18.59
Pleass	15	21	4	274	77*	16.11
Davies (H.)	26	35	4	419	52	13.51
Clay	5	6	0	47	28	7.83
Hever	22	25	10	114	26*	7.60
Griffiths	4	6	2	17	16	4.25
Trick	7	7	3	6	5	1.50

Also batted: Davies (G.) 7, James 17, Lavis 4

	Overs	M	R	W	Avge
Clay	180.2	49	374	27	13.85
Muncer	1082.5	323	2278	139	16.38
Trick	303.5	118	607	36	16.86
Hever	560.2	134	1313	77	17.05
Jones (W.E.)	304.1	61	918	38	24.15
Watkins	440.2	111	910	35	26.00
Wooller	798.1	222	1865	63	29.60
Griffiths	113.2	20	326	8	40.75
Clift	40.5	5	108	0	
Davies (E.)	44	8	117	0	
James	24	4	59	1	
Lavis	3	0	5	1	

1969 – P. 24, W.11, L.O, D.13

	M	I	NO	Runs	HS	Avge
Jones (A.)	24	37	3	1441	122★	42.38
Majid	24	35	1	1302	156	38.29
Lewis (A.R.)	24	36	4	1152	91	36.00
Walker	23	31	9	771	73	35.04
Jones (E.W.)	24	29	8	691	102★	32.90
Davis (B.A.)	24	36	3	956	103	28.96
Davis (R.C.)	24	35	2	773	116	23.42
Nash	21	25	6	435	52	22.89
Cordle	23	30	7	412	56★	17.91
Shepherd	24	18	11	84	33	12.00
Lewis (D.W.)	2	3	1	24	14★	12.00
Williams	21	18	6	109	37★	9.08
Wheatley	6	3	1	3	2★	1.50

	Overs	M	R	W	Avge
Nash	562.1	152	1348	71	18.98
Cordle	401.5	94	1057	52	20.32
Williams	497.3	137	1111	52	21.36
Wheatley	138.5	36	323	15	21.53
David (R.C.)	206	46	545	24	22.70
Shepherd	876	336	1678	69	24.31
Walker	475.2	185	1060	43	24.65
Majid	120	27	247	8	30.87
Lewis (D.W.)	37	6	141	3	47.00
Lewis (A.R.)	1	0	11	0	

1997 – P.17, W.8, L.2 D.7

	M	I	NO	Runs	HS	Avge
James	17	28	4	1605	162	66.87
Maynard	17	23	6	1106	161★	65.05
Morris	16	26	4	1207	233★	54.86
Dale	17	25	3	840	142★	38.18
Croft	13	18	1	577	86	33.94
Evans	1	1	0	31	31	31.00
Cottey	15	19	4	370	76★	24.66
Shaw	17	20	5	352	53★	23.46
Butcher	9	9	1	172	58	21.50
Thomas	16	16	3	258	75★	19.84
Waqar	16	17	2	290	47	19.33
Powell	3	6	2	62	41★	15.50
Watkin	17	16	3	138	39	10.61
Cosker	13	8	5	14	7	4.66

	Overs	M	R	W	Avge
Waqar	441.4	83	1551	68	22.80
Watkin	508.2	143	1393	61	22.83
Croft	504.2	118	1259	54	23.31
Thomas	330.3	49	1160	44	26.36
Butcher	65.4	14	270	8	33.75
Cosker	255.3	62	736	20	36.80
Powell	1	0	3	0	
Cottey	3.3	1	19	0	
Maynard	6.5	0	39	0	
Dale	49.1	11	169	0	

APPENDIX TWO

Hugh Morris's first-class career record for Glamorgan

	M	I	NO	Runs	HS	Avge	100	50
1981	1	2	0	21	16	10.50	0	0
1982	4	6	3	213	63	71.00	0	2
1983	8	14	3	228	34	20.72	0	0
1984	12	20	4	562	114*	33.87	1	4
1985	15	18	4	375	62	26.78	0	1
1986	26	44	2	1522	128*	36.23	2	11
1987	26	48	2	1304	143	28.34	3	4
1988	19	33	3	832	87	27.73	0	6
1989	24	41	2	1299	133	33.30	3	7
1990	25	46	5	2276	160*	55.51	10	10
1991	19	34	7	1644	156*	60.88	5	8
1992	22	36	3	1546	146	46.85	6	5
1993	19	35	2	1326	134*	40.18	5	6
1994	16	31	2	885	106	30.52	1	6
1995	17	31	2	1498	166*	51.66	6	8
1996	17	31	2	1656	202*	57.10	6	9
1997	16	26	4	1207	233*	54.86	4	3

APPENDIX THREE

Hugh Morris's first-class hundreds for Glamorgan

1997	165 v Somerset	(Taunton)
	173 v Gloucestershire	(Sophia Gardens)
	135 v Durham	(Sophia Gardens)
	233*v Warwickshire	(Sophia Gardens)

1996	149 v Essex	(Chelmsford)
	118 v Kent	(Sophia Gardens)
	106 v Leicestershire	(Swansea)
	108 v Gloucestershire	(Bristol)
	202*v Yorkshire	(Sophia Gardens)
	126*v Cambridge University	(Fenners)

1995	104*v Nottinghamshire	(Sophia Gardens)
	166*v Nottinghamshire	(Sophia Gardens)
	106 v Durham	(Swansea)
	114 v Kent	(Tunbridge Wells)
	109 v Northamptonshire	(Sophia Gardens)
	125 v Oxford University	(The Parks)

1994	106 v Sussex	(Hove)

1993	133 v Nottinghamshire	(Swansea)
	102 v Nottinghamshire	(Swansea)
	134*v Yorkshire	(Middlesbrough)
	100 v Derbyshire	(Derby)
	109*v Oxford University	(The Parks)

1992	126 v Durham	(Hartlepool)
	104*v Sussex	(Eastbourne)
	117 v Somerset	(Abergavenny)
	123 v Worcestershire	(New Road)
	104 v Lancashire	(Colwyn Bay)
	146 v Middlesex	(Lord's)

1991	131 v Hampshire	(Southampton)
	156*v Yorkshire	(Headingley)

	156*v Sussex	(Sophia Gardens)
	132 v Northamptonshire	(Sophia Gardens)
	141 v Somerset	(Taunton)
1990	160*v Derbyshire	(Sophia Gardens)
	126 v Sri Lanka	(Ebbw Vale)
	102*v Nottinghamshire	(Worksop)
	110 v Nottinghamshire	(Worksop)
	100 v Middlesex	(Lord's)
	106 v Warwickshire	(Swansea)
	119 v Worcestershire	(Abergavenny)
	102 v Yorkshire	(Sophia Gardens)
	100*v Kent	(Swansea)
	103 v Oxford University	(The Parks)
1989	108 v Warwickshire	(Swansea)
	133 v Warwickshire	(Edgbaston)
	102 v Cambridge University	(Fenners)
1987	143 v Oxford University	(The Parks)
	105 v Warwickshire	(Edgbaston)
	115 v Warwickshire	(Edgbaston)
1986	114 v Worcestershire	(New Road)
	128*v Kent	(Canterbury)
1984	114*v Yorkshire	(Sophia Gardens)

APPENDIX FOUR

Hugh Morris's opening partners

		I	NO	Runs	HS	Avge	100	50
In first-class cricket								
Jones (A.L.)	1985	4	0	26	15	6.50	0	0
Hopkins	1985	34	1	960	133	29.09	1	5
Pauline	1986	16	0	562	104	35.12	1	3
James	1987	177	7	7392	250	43.48	17	38
Butcher (A.R.)	1987	115	4	6592	269	59.38	25	23
Metson	1989	4	0	146	66	36.50	0	1
Cann	1990	4	0	191	120	47.75	1	1
Cottey	1991	2	1	40	31*	40.00	0	0
Maynard	1991	8	0	223	114	27.87	1	0
Dale	1993	17	0	604	238	35.52	1	1
Williams (J.R.A.)	1993	2	0	12	8	6.00	0	0
Hemp	1994	2	0	156	119	79.00	1	0
Dalton	1995	2	0	41	41	20.50	0	0
In one-day cricket								
Hopkins	1983	44	2	1666	143*	39.66	4	6
Jones (A.L.)	1984	7	0	280	109	40.00	1	1
Derrick	1985	1	0	0	0	0.00	0	0
Cottey	1986	3	0	87	76	29.00	0	1
James	1987	91	4	3865	192*	44.43	10	15
Butcher (A.R.)	1987	35	0	1290	123	36.85	4	6
Maynard	1989	17	0	546	95	32.11	0	2
Holmes	1990	3	0	35	24	11.66	0	0
Dale	1990	10	0	257	50	25.70	0	1
Hemp	1996	1	0	7	7	7.00	0	0
Evans	1996	3	0	31	25	10.33	0	0
Croft	1996	9	0	323	79	35.89	0	3
Thomas	1997	1	0	18	18	18.00	0	0
Butcher (G.P.)	1997	1	0	28	28	28.00	0	0

APPENDIX FIVE

Hugh Morris's and Steve James's century opening partnerships for Glamorgan in championship matches

1991	108	v	Hampshire	(Southampton)
1992	250	v	Lancashire	(Colwyn Bay)
	147	v	Surrey	(Neath)
1993	110	v	Sussex	(Sophia Gardens)
1994	125	v	Sussex	(Hove)
1995	147	v	Middlesex	(Colwyn Bay)
	213★	v	Nottinghamshire	(Sophia Gardens)
	113	v	Yorkshire	(Sophia Gardens)
1996	240	v	Gloucestershire	(Bristol)
	103	v	Lancashire	(Sophia Gardens)
	152	v	Nottinghamshire	(Worksop)
	177	v	Hampshire	(Southampton)
	199	v	Essex	(Chelmsford)
1997	190	v	Warwickshire	(Sophia Gardens)
	110	v	Yorkshire	(Headingley)
	229	v	Durham	(Sophia Gardens)
	115	v	Worcestershire	(New Road)

APPENDIX SIX

Glamorgan records

Most successful opening partnerships

	M	Inns	NO	Runs	HS	100	50	Avge
H. Morris–A.R. Butcher	99	115	4	6592	269	25	23	59.38
H. Morris–S.P. James	120	177	7	7392	250	17	38	43.48
A. Jones–J.A. Hopkins	189	230	1	8525	253	14	50	37.24
D.E. Davies–A.H. Dyson	389	439	7	12716	274	32	61	29.92

Leading run-scorers in first-class cricket

			Runs	Avge	100	50
1.	A. Jones	(1957–83)	34596	33.03	52	186
2.	D.E. Davies	(1924–54)	26102	27.85	31	148
3.	W.G.A. Parkhouse	(1948–64)	22619	31.81	32	123
4.	H. Morris	(1981–97)	18520	41.06	52	88
5.	A.H. Dyson	(1926–49)	17920	27.19	24	92
6.	B. Hedges	(1950–67)	17733	25.22	21	84
7.	A.J. Watkins	(1939–61)	17419	30.37	29	89
8.	M.P. Maynard	(1985–97)	16685	44.73	38	94
9.	P.M. Walker	(1956–72)	16510	26.12	12	86
10.	D. Davies	(1923–39)	15008	24.20	16	71
	P.A. Cottey	(1986–97)	9334	39.37	19	50
	S.P. James	(1985–97)	8839	38.60	25	31
	A. Dale	(1989–97)	6898	33.32	14	33
	R.D.B. Croft	(1989–97)	5166	26.91	2	23

Scorers of double centuries in first-class cricket

287★	D.E. Davies	v	Gloucestershire	(Newport)	1939
280★	R.G. Duckfield	v	Surrey	(The Oval)	1936
243	M.P. Maynard	v	Hampshire	(Southampton)	1991
235	S.P. James	v	Nottinghamshire	(Worksop)	1996
233★	H. Morris	v	Warwickshire	(Sophia Gardens)	1997
233	M.J.L. Turnbull	v	Worcestershire	(Swansea)	1937
230★	S.P. James	v	Leicestershire	(Grace Road)	1995
230	J.A. Hopkins	v	Worcestershire	(New Road)	1977

228★	R.C. Fredericks	v	Northamptonshire	(Swansea)	1972
225	J.T. Bell	v	Worcestershire	(Dudley)	1926
224★	I.V.A. Richards	v	Middlesex	(Sophia Gardens)	1993
223	A.R. Lewis	v	Kent	(Gravesend)	1966
216	D. Davies	v	Somerset	(Newport)	1939
215	D.E. Davies	v	Essex	(Brentwood)	1948
214★	A. Dale	v	Middlesex	(Sophia Gardens)	1993
214	M.P. Maynard	v	Lancashire	(Sophia Gardens)	1996
212★	Javed Miandad	v	Leicestershire	(Swansea)	1984
212★	W.E. Jones	v	Essex	(Brentwood)	1948
208	A.H. Dyson	v	Surrey	(The Oval)	1932
207	W.E. Jones	v	Kent	(Gravesend)	1948
205	M.J.L. Turnbull	v	Nottinghamshire	(Arms Park)	1932
204★	R.C. Ontong	v	Middlesex	(Swansea)	1984
204★	A. Jones	v	Hampshire	(Basingstoke)	1980
204	Majid Khan	v	Surrey	(The Oval)	1972
204	M.P. Maynard	v	Nottinghamshire	(Sophia Gardens)	1991
202★	H. Morris	v	Yorkshire	(Sophia Gardens)	1996
201	W.G.A. Parkhouse	v	Kent	(Swansea)	1956
200★	W.E. Bates	v	Worcestershire	(Kidderminster)	1927
200★	M.J.L. Turnbull	v	Northamptonshire	(Swansea)	1935
200★	Javed Miandad	v	Somerset	(Taunton)	1981
200★	Javed Miandad	v	Essex	(Colchester)	1981
200★	Javed Miandad	v	Australia	(Neath)	1985
200★	M.J. Powell	v	Oxford University	(The Parks)	1997